To my incredible wife, JoAnne, who
is responsible for me telling you all my
Skook stories. Many she has heard,
but some will be new to her.

Thanks, Sweetie, as always, for
your support and inspiration.

Introduction

Welcome to the second volume of *Growin' Up Skook*. For the record, I'm as surprised about this as you might be. When my wife, JoAnne, suggested in 2021 that I write a book containing humorous stories about growing up in the small town of Ashland, Schuylkill County, Pennsylvania, in the 1960s, I'll admit I was somewhat apprehensive. Nonfiction wasn't my thing; horror fiction was. Nonetheless, I recognized a good idea when I heard one and agreed, always eager to please my wife. She came up with the concept and even thought of the title *Growin' Up Skook*, and I just did the grunt work.

For anyone unfamiliar with that first book, "The Skook" is a slang term for Schuylkill County. This is because many people, especially locals, mispronounce Schuylkill. Instead of the correct pronunciation, School-kill, they tend to say, Skook-ull. So, a few years ago, someone started referring to Schuylkill County as The Skook. I'm unsure where the nickname originated, but it seemed to have stuck. As a result, those of us who are natives, transplants, or former residents are referred to as "Skooks."

Since writing *Growin' Up Skook* and meeting many people who have enjoyed the book, I've heard varying opinions regarding the Skook moniker. Some people have embraced it, others detest it, and others don't care one way or the other. Since I've been called many worse things than a Skook, I suppose I fall into the category of ambivalence. Either way, the old adage, when applied to Schuylkill County and yours truly, may be accurate. Apparently, you can take the boy out of the Skook, but you can't take the Skook out of the boy.

As JoAnne predicted, the book sold well, and most people who read it said they enjoyed it and had a wonderful time remembering an era long gone by. The greatest surprise to me was how even people with no connection to Schuylkill County, or in some cases, Pennsylvania, enjoyed reading the book. People in other states also

Growin' Up Skook 2: More Stories from "The Skook"

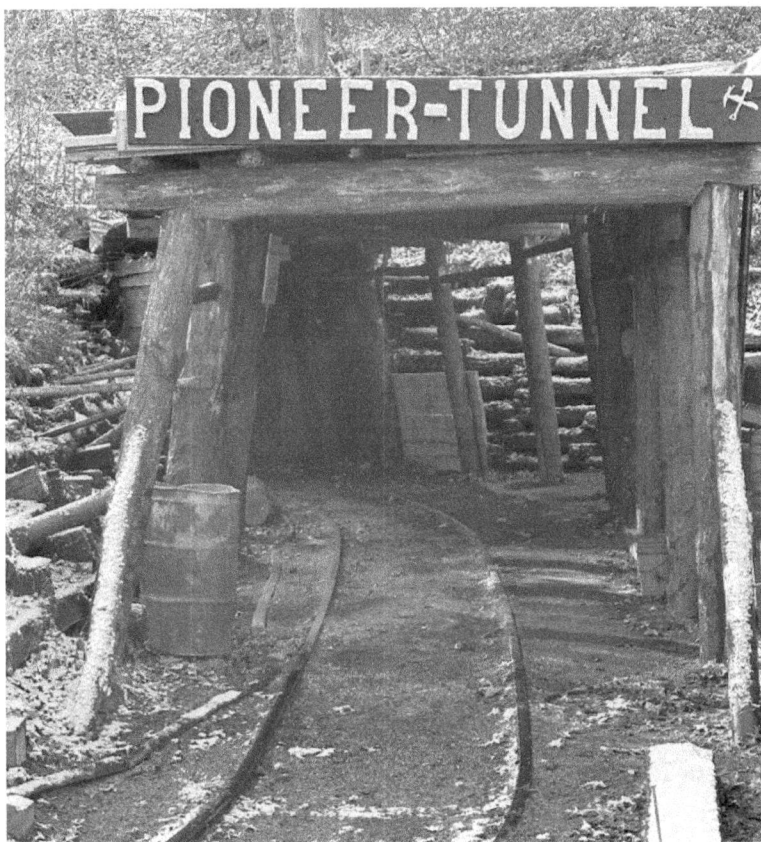

Thomas M. Malafarina

Printed in the United States of America

FIRST EDITION

ISBN: 978-1-952352-29-4

Published by:

Crave Press

www.cravepress.com

loved reading my lighthearted look at small-town life in America in the 1960s. I have always felt the best gift an author can ask for is a reader's precious time. And to have people enjoy your work is more than any writer could hope for. Many of you gave me that gift, and for that, I will be eternally grateful.

If that were not reward enough, many readers wanted more and asked me to write additional stories from my childhood in Ashland. If I felt uncertain about writing the first book, the idea of tackling a second collection made me even more apprehensive. I couldn't dream that a second volume would be as well received as the first. Nevertheless, I had more stories to tell, and readers were asking for them, so I decided to put my concerns aside and bring you *Growin' Up Skook 2: More Stories From the Skook.*

The first *Growin' Up Skook* book was a labor of love from me for my wife at her request. It was also a fun way to pay homage to a place and time that helped mold me into the man I am today. This second book is as well. Both books were also written as an entertaining way to relate my stories to you and hopefully give you, the reader, enjoyment. After all, isn't that what reading is about?

So, as the Good Book says, "Ask, and ye shall receive." I hope you enjoy reading *Growin' Up Skook 2: More Stories From the Skook* as much as I enjoyed writing it. If you are unfamiliar with my first *Growin' Up Skook* book, that's not a problem. I'll do my best to keep you up to speed. If you enjoy this book, I'd highly recommend reading the first as well. For those who have read the first book, I'll try to limit redundancy except where needed or where I simply forgot that I previously mentioned something.

Thomas M. Malafarina

Chapter 1

I woke up that early summer morning on July 24, 1965, having only just turned the ripe old age of ten the previous day. Now that I was no longer living in the single digits, I wondered if my young life would be any different than it had been the day before. I didn't think it would be, and honestly, I didn't need it to be any different or better. I was a happy and contented little guy, satisfied with my home, town, family, and friends.

I wasn't sure what adventures I would have that day, but I knew I would certainly have some since every day was new and overflowing with untapped potential, especially since school was out and I was a kid on summer vacation.

I put on my jeans and a tee shirt, did my morning essentials, and then headed downstairs for a bowl of cereal. Being the first one awake, I made myself my usual bowl of Rice Krispies with lots of milk and sugar. Then I remembered it was Saturday morning. That fact alone would change the direction of my day, or at least my morning. None of the neighborhood kids would be looking for adventure until after lunch because they would all be busy watching Saturday morning cartoons like me. I didn't want to miss Mighty Mouse, Heckel and Jeckel, Tennessee Tuxedo, Rocky and Bullwinkle, The Three Stooges, Little Rascals, or any other favorites. I also enjoyed watching Gene London and his Cartoon Corners General Store show because he could draw in the Disney style, like nobody's business. Besides, there would be plenty of time to go outside later.

Generally, when I left my house in the morning on a typical non-cartoon summer weekday, I knew I wouldn't return until lunchtime. Then, after lunch, I'd be back playing outside with friends until supper time. After supper, I'd go back outside to play again until the street lights came on or my mom called for me to come in for bed. Of course, by "call," I don't mean "call me" on a cell phone since they wouldn't exist for many decades to come. My mom would simply stick her head out the front door and yell my name. Since neither I nor my friends were ever supposed to be more than shouting distance away, I knew I had better be able to hear her call. That was one of the unwritten but never-to-be-violated rules. There were many more rules, and at some time, I'm sure, my friends and I violated most of them repeatedly.

Here's an example of one of those unwritten rules: if your mom didn't call, but one of your friend's mom called him for supper, it meant it was time for all of us to go to our respective homes. It was just something we all knew. When one person's mom called for her kid, it was the same as your mom calling for you. That's simply how things were done, and God help you if you tried to disobey that rule.

None of us was ever dumb enough to stay out later once someone's mom called. We would never think of walking into the house late and saying, "But Mom, Dave's mom called him, but you didn't call me." That simply would never fly. As far as we kids were concerned, all parents belonged to some secret society that made them all equal and on the same team. We were not privy to the workings of that clandestine organization and supposed we never would be until we grew up and became parents ourselves. Then, we might be allowed to join, learn the secret handshake, and suddenly get bestowed with all the knowledge in the universe. We kids didn't know much about how that secret parental club operated, but we knew it was real.

Since every parent was part of this mysterious cabal, we learned to watch our step around any of them. For example, if Charlie or Ron's mom yelled at you for something dumb you did or said, that was the same as if your own mom yelled at you. They were grownups and parents, all members of the same group. If you did something wrong, by the time you got home, your mom would somehow know all about whatever stupid thing you did, all because of that mysterious secret parental network. If you were extra stupid and mouthed off to your friend's mom, you could be guaranteed your mom would find out about it almost instantly. Then, by the time you got home, you were a dead kid walking. This was especially true if your mother gave you the dreaded, "Wait till your father gets home." If you were told that, you might as well order yourself a tombstone.

Usually, while I was watching cartoons, the rest of my family awoke one at a time. Eventually, they would all come downstairs. That meant five other people would all be walking around talking in our small, two-story wood-framed row house. This included my mom, dad, two older sisters, and younger brother. I think living in such tight quarters was how I learned to develop the ability to ignore or shut off external noises. It's one of my superpowers. To this day, I can concentrate in almost any noisy situation. For example, I can work on writing a story while our dogs and cats run around the house barking, hissing, and acting like … well, like animals.

When I eventually decided to finally go out and start my day, I realized I would have to figure out who would join me in whatever adventure awaited me. This was never a matter of picking which friends to play with; it was usually based on whoever happened to be outside. It was pretty much guaranteed you would run into several friends, as we had no shortage of kids in our neighborhood.

The same was true with figuring out what to do. It depended on who was around and what they were hoping to do. For example, I might want to go into the hills behind our neighborhood and build a tree shack. Obviously, this wasn't something I would try to tackle alone, even at the ripe old age of ten. If I wanted to take on a project of that size, I would need several others as that sort of task would require hammers, saws, nails, several kids, and finding lumber.

Luckily, my friend Eric's dad was a carpenter and owned a lumber mill. He also had an open pit where he dumped scrap wood, insulation, and other materials. We never knew what would eventually become of that scrapped material, but we had a pretty good idea of where some of it was heading; it would be confiscated by a group of bored young boys looking to build a tree shack. We never considered taking that stuff stealing, but I suppose it probably was. Likewise, we never thought of the trees in the woods where we were building our shacks belonging to someone, but of course, they did as well. So not only were we thieves, but we were vagrants and squatters. To make matters worse, we were also tree vandals and potential tree killers. It's a wonder our faces weren't on "Wanted" posters in the post office.

Another thing we did that might get us a few checkmarks on the negative side of Saint Peter's ledger on judgment day involved the choice of wallpaper we used inside some of our tree shacks, especially as we got older. Some of the older boys would convince a few of the younger and more innocent-looking of our gang to shoplift dirty magazines, also known to us as skin books, from Leonard's bookstore. Leonard's store had books, magazines, and things like that. In addition, he had a great pinball machine in the back that older kids could blow their hard-earned savings on. He was a kind, gentle soul with more patience than most to tolerate the racket from those rowdy, would-be pinball wizards. Leonard didn't see very well and was often distracted by the noise and misbehavior from the back room. That provided a perfect cover for one of the little thieves to lift a *Playboy* or two.

For the record, I never told any kids to steal any books, and I never stole any myself; however, I did hear about this nefarious activity from one of the other guys, and I did help wallpaper our shacks with naked pictures, the spoils of that pilfering. (I was only human.) Still, I have to think that even being only peripherally involved with stealing from a near-blind man might require some serious penance on my part at some point in the future; in other words, when I'm cramming for that final spiritual exam.

Thank goodness no adults knew about what we were doing, or if they did, maybe they chose to ignore it. Perhaps they thought it was a good way to keep us out of more serious trouble. Speaking of serious trouble, we eventually had to abandon our forest structures after finding paper bags with dried Tester's glue in the bottom scattered

4

inside. This meant that older boys, likely local high school psychopaths, were using our shacks for sniffing glue, and God only knew what else. So, whenever signs of these future death row inmates would appear, we'd bail and eventually build another shack elsewhere.

But suppose you wanted to build a tree shack, and you happen to meet up with two or three other friends who wanted to play pickup baseball in the street? Then the shack would wait, and baseball would take priority. Or maybe it was too hot to play outside, and someone suggested a cool place to hang out, like an area behind our neighborhood that we called "The Pines." That place was next to the Ashland High School and was thick with large pine trees that virtually kept all sunlight out. It was an ideal place to sit, hang out, and talk. Sometimes, we'd discuss the latest movies at the Roxy Theater downtown or maybe some horror movies we saw on TV or at the Saturday matinees. During the hot summer, empty coal bins under our porches also made a cool, shady place to hang out.

I remember the previous summer when one of my friends received an old hand-me-down fishing rod from an uncle or somebody, and we got this ingenious idea to go fishing. Keep in mind none of us knew the first thing about catching fish. In addition, we had nowhere nearby to fish. We considered walking uptown to the ice skating pond near Eureka Park. It was July, so the pond wouldn't be frozen. But we weren't sure if it had any fish in it anyway. I knew it sometimes had frogs because several of us had pulled apart what we called "double-deckers," which, we learned many years later, had been frogs that were in the process of mating. Talk about ruining somebody's good time. Such are the hazards of being a dumb kid.

Someone suggested we go to Coney Island (or Cooney Island, depending on your pronunciation preference), which was a larger pond located just off the road between Ashland and Gordon. The pond was so polluted from mine seepage that parts were orange with sulfur. Nonetheless, we were desperate to try fishing so off we went. This was a good hike, several miles (well out of shouting distance), so we had to time things so we would be back before the call for supper.

We arrived at the pond and threw the fishing line into the water. We didn't know about casting, so throwing was the best we could accomplish. There was some sort of metal thing-a-ma-jig at the end, which one of the guys called a sinker, which helped the line go out pretty far. We also knew from TV shows, like Andy of Mayberry, that we needed some sort of bait. Nobody had any, and there weren't any worms around, so we just winged it. Needless to say, we sat for about an hour and had no bites. We decided to leave when one of the guys saw a dead, bloated, rotting fish floating on top of the water near some downed tree branches. We were so desperate to catch something that we tried unsuccessfully to snag the disgusting specimen with the rod so we wouldn't have to go home empty-handed. But in the end, cooler heads prevailed, and we simply returned to our neighborhood.

Other times, we might also decide to make a haunted fun house in the garage rec room of our friends Dale and Kris. They were the only family in the neighborhood with a garage, and one of the bays had been converted into a playroom. We spent many hot days hanging out in that room and often planned how to set up a haunted house to scare all the neighborhood kids, which we usually did. It was cool hearing the neighborhood girls squeal in fright.

The key to having a successful summer adventure always started with finding someone to play with. If you hadn't gotten past that first step, your day might have been quite boring indeed. Thankfully, most of my friends had parents who were no more financially well off than my folks, so few took off on vacations and they could usually be counted on to be looking for someone to hang with just as much as I was.

My friend Ronny lived in the row house next to ours, and since our houses were old, wood-framed dwellings, they didn't have firewalls between them. This meant you could place your ear against the wall of the adjacent house and hear if anyone was awake and

6

moving around. When Ronny's cousins from uptown visited, it sounded like a riot was going on next door. He called his cousins "the Indians" because of their wild behavior. He often said, "The Indians are stopping by tonight, so get ready." This was his way of warning me it would be a noisy evening and that I might want to turn up the volume on the TV.

Ronny and I had taken the idea of hearing what went on next door a step further, and at the bottom-right corner of the shared wall in our back rooms, which happened to be mine and my brother's bedroom, we had managed to create a small hole about one-quarter inch round that went from my house to his. This allowed us to converse through the hole at night or early in the morning.

I often would bend down and put my ear to the hole to listen for the sounds of anyone awake. If I heard nothing, it meant everybody was still asleep next door, so my only option would be to go out into the world and see who was out and about. Do I recall what I did that day after my tenth birthday or how it turned out? No, not really. But I can assume that I walked around the neighborhood looking for other kids who might be out doing the same thing. The chances are pretty good that I found at least one other friend since we all knew about our summer routines. I can also assume that as the day progressed, more kids started dribbling out of their houses to join the rest of us. This was how it was for us as kids in the 1960s while we were "growin' up Skook."

Chapter 2

In the 1950s and 1960s, Ashland, Pennsylvania, was a great place to be a kid and a great town to grow up in. It was a typical Schuylkill County, coal region town with primarily wood-framed row houses and a nice mixture of European ethnicities such as Irish, German, Italian, Polish, Lithuanian, and many others.

As I mentioned, my family and I lived at the end of a group of four row houses about twelve feet wide with a first-floor parlor, living room, and kitchen. Upstairs, we had three small bedrooms and a bathroom. We had no basement but had a two-room "cellar." My dad, my brother, and I eventually dug out under the kitchen to make a third cellar room. The motivation for this cellar extension was to eliminate the influx of rats and water bugs (cockroaches) into our kitchen cabinets.

Things were always a bit tight in our house with my two parents, George Malafarina and Lois (Metzinger) Malafarina, my two older sisters, Louiseann (Weezie) and Georgine (Jeanie), and myself and my younger brother, George, all sharing the limited space. The girls shared one bedroom, and George and I shared another.

George and I are four years apart in age. In fact, all of us Malafarina kids are four years apart. Jeanie is four years older than me, and Louise is four years older than Jeanie. Louise and I are eight years apart, born on the same day, July 23. Who could ask for a better birthday present than to get a baby brother like me? Okay, maybe a bike might be better, but not nearly as cute.

One thing I will always remember fondly about my childhood was supper time when my dad would get home from work, and somehow, all six of us would fit around our metal and Formica-topped kitchen table for our evening meal, which we shared together every night without fail. I never would have considered suggesting that I might take my meal into the living room so I could watch TV. Stuff like that just wasn't something you even dared to think about.

The only exception was if I were sick with a cold or flu. Then, I would be confined to the couch in the living room with a metal folding tray table for my food, comic books, and whatever else might make me feel better. Otherwise, it was supper at the table with the family. I feel bad for many kids nowadays who no longer benefit from the entire family sitting around the dinner table discussing their day. Although these were times when I often got yelled at for joking or saying goofy things to make my sister, Jeanie, laugh, they were also special times when the whole family was together.

At mealtime, I learned so much about my dad's coworkers, older sisters' classmates, and friends that, although I had never met most of them, I had formed images of them. This proved interesting when I eventually had teachers in school that my sisters previously talked about. Before I ever met a teacher, I knew many things about them, most of which were negative, such as which teachers were mean, which were nice, which were boozers, which were quick to paddle, and which had hairy legs and bad breath. I knew their nicknames, like Birdie Legs, Bomar Brain, Barracuda Breath, Giddy, and Widdy. I knew which teachers were easy graders and which were the tough ones.

Most of the time, I listened carefully to the conversations so that I could learn, but sometimes, when the spirit moved me, I would say something goofy and make Jeanie laugh. I can't recall what I might have done or said, but I always knew I succeeded when Jeanie laughed, and Mom said, "Don't encourage him." My dad would usually just yell at me and call me "class clown." I could tell by the tone of his voice it was meant to be an insult, but I had never thought of it that way. I liked making people laugh. One of my older cousins was voted class clown in the yearbook senior superlatives section. For some reason, that always made my dad angry, and he wanted to make sure I didn't follow in those footsteps.

I have plenty of food-related memories from those younger days; some were good, some were great, and some weren't all that wonderful. I should point out that I was and still am a ridiculously picky eater. I'm one of those weirdos who is what I call "texture sensitive." That means if I don't like how a particular food feels in my mouth, I won't eat it. The same thing is true with smells. If I don't like how food smells, I won't even try to taste it. As if that's not bad enough, if I don't like the color of a particular food, I won't eat it either. Oh, yeah, I forgot. If I don't like the name of the food, there's no way I will give it a second look. So something like guacamole loses on just about all the above criteria. Yeah, I know it's weird, but I've learned to live with it, thanks to Italian foods and an extremely patient and caring wife.

My mom was, for the most part, a great cook, especially when it came to my favorite Italian dishes, such as spaghetti and meatballs or lasagna. This was quite an accomplishment for a girl of German descent. Mom also flawlessly cooked my other favorites: chicken, sausage, turkey, filling, gravy, beef roast, meatloaf, mac and cheese. Mom was an excellent baker, and her cakes, pies, and fudge were the stuff of legend.

One of my favorite memories was being allowed to scrape the bowl and mixer beaters after Mom made her delicious chocolate fudge. It inspired one of my favorite old-guy dumb jokes. When someone asks if my mom let me lick the beaters when she was baking, I like to say, "Sure, and occasionally, she'd even turn off the mixer first." See, I told you it was dumb.

Despite her talent as a baker and cook, even my mom had a few clunkers. Pork chops and steak were two meals that told an entirely different story. George Washington's men at Valley Forge had less trouble eating shoe leather than they would have with my mom's pork chops. These meals, along with other things I hated like fish, potato soup, and all cabbage-based meals, were responsible for my spending many nights after everyone had left the table crying while

11

trying to force down food I hated that had grown cold. This is why, as an adult, I never eat anything I don't want to.

I grew tired of hearing my parents' lectures about the kids starving in China who would kill for a chance to have the food I hated. If only my parents would have known that in 30 to 40 years, those same Chinese kids would grow up to be adults taking all the jobs most parents hated. Maybe when I heard a group of relatives complaining ad nauseam about their jobs, I should have said, "You know, workers in China are starving for your jobs and would kill for them." I think my assessment would have been every bit as accurate as their food analogy, although if I had spoken up, it probably wouldn't have been appreciated.

Holiday dinners, whether turkey and stuffing ("filling" in Skookspeak) or baked ham, were also excellent. Sometimes, we would set up our dining table in the middle room for holiday meals and invite my aunts or grandmother over. My paternal grandmother, Lydia Texter Malafarina, died before I was born, and my paternal grandfather, Pietro Malafarina, died when I was about twelve.

My grandparents on the Metzinger side of the family lived in an apartment on South Tenth Street. My grandfather, Robert Metzinger, lost a leg in a mining accident before I was born and seldom left their apartment except to walk on crutches down to the Eagles Social Club on the corner of South Ninth and Centre Streets. My grandmother was a waitress at the Marko Town House on the corner of North Ninth and Centre, so she often would walk the few blocks to our house.

Back in the 1960s, Ashland had a busy downtown shopping district, and it was common for people to walk around town freely, going from store to store and then walking home without worrying about getting robbed or threatened. Those sorts of criminal activities were a rare occurrence back in what was described as more innocent times. Everybody knew everybody and watched out for each other. My grandmother thought nothing of walking to and from her apartment to the Marko Town House for her shift. Sadly, I fear the same situation might not exist today.

The Marko Town House, formerly known as the Hotel Loper and which is now a building for the elderly, had a feature that could be a source of wonder and adventure for any young boy with a bit of patience and the desire to find some much-needed cash.

All along the North Ninth Street side of "The Marko," as we called it, were a series of metal grates. I believe there may have been three or four of them. What their purpose was, I didn't know or care about as a youngster. I knew that people constantly walked back and forth along North Ninth Street, which was often busy with downtown shoppers who occasionally would stop by the Marko to have lunch or dinner. As they walked, talked, and fiddled with their purses and wallets, sometimes they dropped things like coins, which fell into the grates covering a space about three feet deep. Whether or not the people were aware of their clumsiness, the result was that pennies, nickels, dimes, and sometimes even quarters would find their way to the bottom space below the grates.

This is where patience, timing, and bubble gum joined forces to help provide this particular young boy with much-needed funds. The best time to do what I'll explain next was early morning before pedestrian and automobile traffic was active.

First, I would find a long stick or tree branch. If I was lucky and had planned ahead, I might have a wooden dowel rod from a worn-out mop or broom that I had sawed off the business end. Next, I would chew a good-sized wad of bubblegum until all the "goodie" was out of it. This step was critical. There was an unwritten rule concerning chewing bubble gum. You only chewed it until all the sweet flavor, also known as "goodie," was gone. If you threw it away too early, you wasted good gum and, therefore, good money. If you continued to chew it after the flavor was gone, then it was said you were "chewing your own spit." No one ever mentioned that we were, in essence, chewing our own spit all along the process, but that's an

13

argument for another day. That being said, there was that "sweet spot" just after the "goodie" was gone when the gum had the perfect texture, consistency, and stickiness to allow me to move on to the next step.

This step involved placing the ABC (already been chewed) gum on the end of the stick, making sure it was firmly stuck and wouldn't fall off with vigorous motion. This could be determined by making a series of jerky, thrusting motions similar to a medieval knight in training. If the gum stayed in place, I knew I was ready to go fishing.

This could be determined by making a series of jerky, thrusting motions similar to a medieval knight in training.

Next, I would head down North Ninth Street to the first Marko Townhouse grate and look inside for lost treasure. If I saw anything of interest, I would carefully feed the stick through a grate opening, hover over the item, and then carefully lower it until the gum came in contact with the potential treasure. Once secured, I would slowly raise the stick out of the grate, step to the side, and remove the item, hopefully a significant coin. It was important to step to the side to ensure the treasure didn't fall off and back into the hole, or the process would have to be repeated.

This could usually be done several times until the gum became so encrusted with debris that a new piece had to be used. Although this might be a bit frustrating and could delay the collection process, at least it meant I got to chew another piece of gum, being sure to adhere to the "goodie vs. spit" rule.

This might give some people the idea that I was destined to be a homeless dumpster diver in adulthood, but somehow, I managed to avoid that fate. I was, however, a habitual garbage picker when I was a young boy. Perhaps that's why I thought riding on the back of a garbage truck might be the coolest job ever. My dad often told people how, as he drove me around town, I would shout, "Look, Dad, they have great garbage." He, of course, would never stop.

I had been known to raid the trash of local pharmacies and pick up "neat bottles," which were glass pill bottles, most empty but some not. I often wish I had those old bottles today, as they might be valuable. I recall my mom getting angry with me once when I came home with a box of used hypodermic needles from a local doctor's trash. I now know why it disturbed her, but I didn't know then. I saw them as props for playing mad scientist. My concerned parents had many reasons to worry about their son's future.

Although I have, for the most part, given up digging in the trash for hidden treasures, occasionally, when driving by an interesting pile of rubbish at the curb for collection, I get an itch to investigate. This, however, is an itch that I do not scratch. If I had chosen to live in a more rural environment instead of living in a home in a subdivision, I would probably have a barn filled with the spoils of my garbage picking. Thankfully, however, the size and location of my house and the vigilance of my wife, JoAnne, have joined forces to prevent me from such activities. For example, it's common when we drive around the development for her to catch me looking longingly at someone's trash, and I hear JoAnne say, "Forget it! It's garbage!" Some women have to worry about their husbands looking at other women. Mine has to worry about me ogling "good garbage."

Still, those early days of growing up with little money but lots of creative ideas, to this day, make me want to take trash and turn it into something special. If I had a nickel for every time in my life from childhood to today that I said, "I can make something out of that," I'd be a wealthy man. Such is the legacy of my hometown and "growin' up Skook."

Chapter 3

My family was not rich by any stretch of the imagination, and we often struggled to be lower middle class. This wasn't a big deal since most families in our blue-collar town were in the same financial situation. However, regardless of our money status, my mom always ensured we were clean. That might sound like a strange statement, but it was a concept drilled into all of us Malafarina siblings all our lives. My mom was a firm believer in the notion that simply because someone might be poor or struggling, that was not an excuse to be dirty. Being clean didn't cost much, and it showed that you had personal pride.

Clothing could be washed, even if that meant soaking it in a metal tub and hanging it on a clothesline to dry. If you could afford the luxury, a manual ringer washer could be kept in the cellar, and the ringer could squeeze most of the water out of the clothes, making them dry faster on the clothesline.

My mom was a stickler for being concerned about looking our best despite our low income. She constantly taught us to always be our best and, most importantly, be true to ourselves. We needed to be clean, well-dressed, and always put our best foot forward. Although she taught us to be independent, she stressed that trying to see what others thought of us was important.

She had an old Irish expression she learned as a kid, which she often told us. It was, "Would some power the Giver 'gee us [give us], to see ourselves as others see us. To thine own self be true." In other words, life would be easier if God allowed us to see ourselves as others saw us. The most important aspect of that is "to thine own self be true."

For example, maybe you want to grow up to be the greatest basketball player that ever lived. You love basketball, play it a lot, and you're pretty good. But your mom is five feet tall, and your dad is only about five feet, seven inches. Everyone on your team is taller than you. If you are being true to yourself, you will know you can never be the greatest basketball player in the world. By the time you reach high school, you might not even be good enough to make the basketball team. That doesn't mean you can't continue to play. You just have to realize what other people already know. No matter how much you play or practice or how good you are, you will never be the greatest, and there's nothing wrong with that. Enjoy yourself and have fun, but be realistic. To thine own self be true.

Before my parents could afford an electric washer and dryer, they owned one of those ridiculous but necessary ringer washers. They kept it down in the cellar near our Heatrola coal-fired furnace. Mom hung clothes on clotheslines down there during the winter and outside when the weather was milder.

Always curious and wanting to understand how things worked, I went to the cellar one day to check out the ringer washer when no one was around. It had a large tub for washing clothes and two hard-rubber rollers with a hand crank for squeezing the excess water out so the clothes would dry faster. Unfortunately, I discovered I had no wet clothing to test it out.

At this point in the experiment, any rational person with even an ounce of common sense might think of getting an old rag or handkerchief, wetting it thoroughly, and then using it to run through the rollers. The keywords here are "rational" and "common sense." Being a dumb little kid, I decided putting my index finger between the rollers was a perfect way to test the thing out. Let's just say, on a scale of one to ten, the pain level was an eleven. Fortunately, I figured out how to reverse the rollers before my finger was permanently crushed or broken. It was a little bruised and hurt for about a week, which I hid quite well as it obviously wasn't something I would have wanted to tell anyone about. As the saying goes, "If you're gonna be dumb, you better be tough."

This was similar to when I was about seven or eight and was helping my dad do some work at my mom's cousin's house. As was often the case, I was bored and fooling around with my dad's manual metal staple gun. Suddenly, I was hit with an ingenious inspiration. Why not take the staple gun and shoot a staple into the nearby electric outlet? It made sense to me; after all, the two slots in the outlet had the same approximate spacing as the two prongs on the staple in the gun. It looked like a perfect fit, so why not give it a go?

I learned several things that day. I discovered that a metal staple shot into an electric outlet can cause some amazing sparks, almost like fireworks. Also, for some reason, all the lights and appliances all over the house seemed to turn off simultaneously. I heard a lot of swearing in the other room, and someone saying

19

something called a "fuse" must have blown. Oh yeah, I should also mention that was the first time in my life that I became airborne like Superman for a few seconds, although I doubt his head ever roared like mine did that day. Thank goodness when the adults saw what I did, they were too happy to see me not flashing like a neon bar sign so they could yell at me. I should also point out that I was clean. My mom would have been proud.

While we are on the subject of electricity, did you ever wonder how that single skinny strand of fence wire keeps those big, strong cows and bulls from running away? I wondered that, too. When I was about ten and hanging out with my friend, Ronny, at the dairy where his mom worked, I asked myself that very question. Note to self: don't grab that silly, skinny strand of fence wire because that familiar roar will go up your arm, down through your body, and into your head in about a half second. Oh, and once again, you'll get to fly like Superman. At least my mom would have been happy that just before that experiment, I was clean, and my hair was combed neatly. Unfortunately, that was only until I landed on my butt in the dirt with my hair sticking up in all directions.

When I was a little kid, my younger brother and I used to get a bath together in our huge claw-foot cast iron tub every Saturday night. I don't know if this was to save water or if it was so I could watch out for my brother. This was usually a bubble bath with Avon bubble soap and usually lasted until we couldn't make any more bubbles, or the water got cold. We were never in a hurry to get out because that usually meant we had to go downstairs and sit through the torture of watching the Lawrence Welk show until bedtime. I can tell you that that show was not the Wonderful World of Disney.

Once while bathing, I taught George how to make our own bubbles by farting in the water. However, that didn't go over very well since the smell always lingered way too long in the water for some reason. There was also the risk of producing an over-enthusiastic bit of flatulence, complete with something a bit more substantial ... and solid. That would not be good! This is a teachable moment; torpedoes are bad, or would it be tor-poo-does?

My mom also worried about our hair. She hated seeing kids with unwashed or messy hair. Over the summer, George and I usually got crew cuts, so there wasn't really any combing required. However, when school started and the weather turned cold, we'd have haircuts that needed a nice, straight part and slicked back wave in the front. This meant that every day before school, Mom would give us the once-over, and if our part wasn't perfect and our hair was not properly combed, she'd comb it for us.

I didn't mind that too much because it meant one less thing I had to bother with myself. I just sat in a chair in the kitchen and let Mom do her thing. What I could never understand, however, was why Mom insisted on combing our hair before bed every night. I used to argue that there was no point in combing our hair at night since it would just get messed up when we slept. But in Mom's logic, this was something she had to do.

So, every day, we would go to school looking like our family had more money than we did. That goes back to being concerned about how others saw and thought of us. That was one lesson I really didn't want to learn because it seemed like a lot of work to me. I wanted to be the person who couldn't care less about what others thought. As an adult, I often say I don't care, as if trying to convince myself that I really don't. But those lessons of my youth were drilled into my head, and unfortunately, I have never been able to let them go. I still check my appearance before going anywhere; I shower daily (sometimes twice daily), check my clothes to make sure they are appropriate, and keep my mustache and beard trimmed and the rest of my face shaved. We maintain our house and our vehicles as well. So, I guess the lesson stuck big time. Thanks a lot, Mom.

Chapter 4

I'm willing to admit I was not always a dog or cat lover. Until recently, within the past eight years, the best description of my relationship with pets in general might be reluctant acceptance. I often wondered why this might be. I'm not a bad person and would never think of doing anything to hurt another living creature; I neither hunt nor fish. All my life, I've met people who feel their lives would be significantly lacking if they didn't have their favorite pet to share that life with them. I was envious of them because I did not seem to have that need and couldn't understand why. If my wife or the kids wanted a pet, I would go along with the idea, but always from a distance, never getting too close. It wasn't until I wrote this chapter that I realized how my many unfortunate interactions with animals as a young boy may have affected me well into adulthood.

Growing up in Ashland in the 1960s, many, if not most, kids I knew in town had pets. These were not what might be considered more exotic pets like snakes, lizards, guinea pigs, gerbils, or the like. It seemed most kids either had a dog or a cat. Few had both. I'm not exactly sure why this was, but it was likely related to expense. Most of the pets I knew about were not purebreds but were what locals sometimes called "Heinz 57 varieties" or "Who Done Its?" Few people ever paid for dogs or cats. Since spaying and neutering was about as unheard of in our small town as was taking your pet to a veterinarian, there was always an abundance of dogs and cats free for the taking.

We never could have even dreamed of a day when we might consider purchasing pet medical insurance. There were no formal pet adoption centers where you were scrutinized under the probing eyes of animal rescue organization volunteers who asked more personal questions than were likely carried out during the Spanish Inquisition. The process back then was much simpler. Johnny's cat had kittens, and Sally's dog had puppies. Want one? Take it.

An unfortunate but apparently financially necessary common practice involved keeping the pet only as long as it remained healthy. If it became sick, there would be no vet visit. Vets cost money. Money was scarce, and free dogs and cats were everywhere. Your pet either got better, or it didn't. That might sound harsh or cruel looking back from where we are today, but that's how things were, and sadly, that was the environment in which I was raised.

Pets were pets. Animals were animals. We did not personify pets as many people do today. The only animal personification was done in Saturday morning cartoons or Disney movies. No one referred to dogs and cats as fur babies. When pets passed away, they didn't cross the magical "Rainbow Bridge" into pet Nirvana the way people like to pretend today. They just died, plain and simple. If you wanted a replacement pet, you just asked around town, and by the end of the day, you would have a new kitten or puppy.

The way many people dealt with seriously ill dogs or cats was to find someone who owned a gun and was willing to shoot the ailing critter for them. As things worked out, my dad owned a .22 caliber rifle and would often be called upon to perform this unpleasant bit of business.

Dad and I often used that rifle for target shooting when I was a little older. I should explain that the word "target" is a somewhat generous description. We didn't own classy paper targets or belong to a shooting range or gun club. We did all of our shooting in abandoned strip mines located behind the high school baseball field behind our house. These giant wounds cleaved in the Earth were remnants of the old strip-mining days and, in the 1950s and 1960s, were used as dumping grounds for just about any type of trash imaginable, from small household appliances to larger appliances like stoves and refrigerators to automobiles and just about everything in between.

Our "targets" were whatever we could find. Sometimes, we would use discarded jars, soda, and beer bottles; if we got lucky, we might discover some almost intact plates or bowls. The rats that

24

roamed "the strippins," which was what we called these former strip mines between Ashland and Centralia, were also fair game, although I can't recall either of us having any luck hitting any of the fast-moving creatures in their most unnatural habitat. As I mentioned earlier, Dad reluctantly became the de facto neighborhood canine executioner because he owned a gun and could shoot well.

Although he was not fond of doing this gruesome task, my dad had a big heart and was generous to a fault. He was always eager to help a neighbor in need and couldn't stand to see a terminally ill animal suffer. As such, Dad was often called upon to perform this unpleasant job.

The term "pets" in 1960s Schuylkill County was a less accurately defined description since animals, in general, were treated much differently than we treat them today. Many animals were not well trained, regularly bathed or groomed, vaccinated, or licensed. Many dogs and cats were allowed to roam the town unleashed and sometimes were hit and nearly fatally injured by cars or, in some cases, became the victims of other, more aggressive animals. Dad was called on to reluctantly provide a final solution when this happened.

My first dog was solid black and part Beagle, combined with whatever unknown mixed breed happened to gain the favor of his mother. He, of course, was a freebie, and I named him Blackie. I loved that puppy as much as any little kid could, even though I might not have been very clever when naming pets in my youth. He's a solid black dog, I think I'll name him Blackie. Duh! Then again, several years ago, my wife, JoAnne, and I had a purebred Jack Russel Terrier who we gave the less-than-creative name Jack. So, what can I say?

One day, Blackie got out of our yard and was run over by a truck and was killed. I remember someone telling me he had been hit by a furniture truck making a delivery. I can't recall who told me this, but whoever it was, I believed them. To be completely honest, I have no idea if that account of Blackie's death was even true. All I knew was my puppy whom I loved; he was dead, and I was devastated.

I was told the carpeting and furniture store that owned the truck that ran over Blackie was called "Pinko Carpeting and Furniture." The owners were well-respected, hard-working local folks; they weren't evil pet assassins bent on bringing heartbreak to little boys wherever possible. Even if the account of Blackie's death had been accurate and it had been their truck, I'm certain it wouldn't have been the driver's fault. If anyone was to blame, it was us for allowing the poor little guy to roam free. Blackie's death had been nothing more than an unfortunate accident, for which I'm sure the driver must have felt terrible. I know it affected me greatly.

If I had been older, I might have understood and accepted his passing for the unfortunate accident it was. But try explaining such a concept to a dumb, heartbroken little six- or seven-year-old whose dog had just been killed. I wanted revenge. I was out for blood. I had seen enough Westerns to know about vengeance. However, I wasn't a gunslinging cowboy and, as such, had little recourse for seeking justice for my poor slain doggy. Then, one day, the opportunity for revenge came my way. While walking on Centre Street, in the business part of town, perhaps on my way to school, I came upon the storefront for the allegedly murderous carpeting and furniture store, whose delivery truck had so callously killed my puppy.

This nexus between myself and the supposed puppy killers was completely unplanned, and I can only assume it was a gift from the universe, and as such, it was meant to be. At last, vengeance would be mine. I stood defiantly in front of the store's door and shouted my curse at the top of my lungs. I screamed, "Pink Nose!" Wow, what a scathing insult!

Yes, that was my curse upon them. I cleverly took the store and family's name and turned it into what I felt was an undeniably horrendous blasphemy, akin to bringing a plague upon the Pinko family and their business. I honestly believed this proclamation on my part not only conveyed my disgust with what had happened but would bring down their vile and murderous house of cards once and for all.

However, today, with the benefit of more intelligent and rational hindsight, I feel I am safe in assuming a few things. First, chances are extremely good that no one inside the store ever heard a word I said. If, by chance, they happened to glance out the window, they would have seen me in my bizarre gyrations and soundless insults. They likely would have ignored me and returned to whatever carpeting or furniture work they had been doing. Passers-by, however, probably gave me a wide birth along the sidewalk, thinking I might have been a bit "soft in the head." For years, I lived with the idea that I had gotten my well-deserved revenge, as only a dumb little kid could imagine.

Most of the neighborhood dogs had pens or dog houses outside. The last dog we had was a white and brown-spotted dog that I cleverly named "Spot." (Yeah, I know, creative genius.) He had a dog house in our small fenced-in yard, but during the coldest months of winter and the hottest months of summer, Spot stayed in our cellar, only going out in the yard to complete his essential business. Spot could have been the poster child for "Who Done It," being part Beagle, and God only knew what else. I can only assume we got him for free from one of my dad's friends.

Spot often escaped the yard and roamed around town, likely making little "Spots" and getting into fights with other would-be suitors. He always came home, until one day, he didn't. Witnesses claimed that he had been picked up by police cruising the neighborhood. It was reported that in the process of being captured, Spot, it was said, bit one of the officers. We don't know if that report was true or not, but my dad decided it would be best not to inquire further, as there would likely be fines and medical bills we couldn't afford to incur. Even if we were able to pay such medical bills, Spot would have likely been euthanized, which was another expense we couldn't afford. He was just a dog, and dogs were everywhere. That was a lesson that seemed to be drilled into us as kids.

Spot wasn't the smartest pick of the litter, and unlike the two dogs my wife and I have today, he was never considered or treated like a member of the family. He just sort of existed. As I mentioned, he lived in our cellar, and the only time he was in the family part of our house was when we opened the kitchen and cellar doors simultaneously, and he ran through the dining room and kitchen to either go out into the yard in the morning or back into the cellar at night.

When Spot escaped the backyard, he would often return battered and bloodied from an altercation with some other critter. Spot never saw a vet, and we never worried about him catching rabies; in hindsight, that probably might have been a prudent course of action, although not an affordable one. Whenever Spot came home after a fight, my dad would wash out his wounds and apply one antiseptic or another. Spot would usually lay around in the cellar for a few days, then he'd be ready to rock and roll all over again. We understood and accepted what would happen to him if he hadn't gotten better and seemed to get worse. Dogs and cats were free, and bullets weren't expensive.

Some of my friends had cats, although it seemed dogs were the primary species of choice. One cat that immediately comes to mind was my neighbor's female cat. To say this cat was the neighborhood trollop would be an understatement. This feline floozie roamed the neighborhood, getting down and funky with any Tomcat she might encounter, including the roaming bands of large, feral mountain cats that came down in packs from "the strippins" looking for a little sumptin-sumptin.

It seemed this cat was perpetually pregnant, and every time she delivered a litter, it always ended badly for them. As a young boy, I witnessed several unfortunate and gruesome incidents involving these kittens, and I wish I hadn't, as they haunt me to this day. These events affected my young, impressionable soul deeply in ways I didn't realize until many years later in adulthood. I won't go into details about these

28

horrible encounters as they were very gory and emotionally troubling for me and would just be disturbing to any pet-loving reader. Suffice it to say, I never participated in any of these horrid occurrences, but unfortunately, I witnessed more than my share.

Dogs were another problem area for me. As a paperboy, I had multiple run-ins with unleashed and vicious dogs. One particularly viscous German shepherd along my paper route was allowed to run free, and it terrorized me to the point that even today, I am not a fan of the breed. I feel bad about that, but I can do little about it. This dog was a beast, a monster. It was massive and looked more like a wolf than a dog. It nearly got me several times, and had I not seen it coming and sought shelter behind another neighbor's iron fence, I hate to think what it might have done to me. I had no idea what I would do as I had to keep delivering papers on that street. Every day became a survival of the fittest challenge, with me being the least fit in the game. It freaked me out so badly that one day, I went home and built the ultimate in canine defense, which I called my "Dog Destroyer."

The weapon was a sawed-off section of an old broom handle about twenty-four inches long. I cut that section in half length-wise. I put a spiked nail on one end of the twelve inch half of the thing, tapping it firmly into the wood, then used a file to sharpen the point. On the second piece, I drilled a hole the same size as the diameter of the nail. This allowed me to insert the spiked end into the hole and have what looked like a twenty-four inch long section of the broom handle. I concealed it nicely in my canvas newspaper bag and positioned it for easy access. When I needed it, I could simply slip it from the bag and pull the sections apart, having a weapon in each hand, one with a sharp spike.

I never wanted to use the weapon and, fortunately, never had to, but keeping that Dog Destroyer tucked safely into my newspaper bag with easy access gave me the confidence, false as it might be, to continue to deliver my papers. Lucky for me, the German shepherd

29

never came after me again. I suspect if he had attacked me, the result would have been less than desirable for me, not for him.

When needed, I could simply pull the two sections of the Dog Destroyer apart, having a weapon in each hand, one with a sharp spike.

Because of how I witnessed animals being treated in my youth and my encounters with stray dogs while delivering my papers, I had trouble getting close to or affectionate with animals. It is also possible that subconsciously, I felt I didn't have the right to a pet's affection. Maybe I feared getting too close to something so vulnerable and fragile could only end badly for me as it had so many times before. I think this was the direct result of all the animals I lost and saw killed as a young boy. I suppose that I hoped if I didn't get too close, I wouldn't be hurt.

This was a false hope since, as an adult, when any of our pets grew old and infirm and eventually had to be euthanized at our veterinarian's office, I realized the errors in my logic. When a pet passed, it hurt me as much as if I had allowed myself to be close to them. It took me far too many years to realize this, but I have finally put those negative childhood memories aside and have, I hope, changed for the better.

Nowadays, we have two dogs that visit our vet more often than I see my doctor, and they get professionally groomed more often than I get haircuts. Between groomings, they are bathed at home, and JoAnne brushes them and removes knots in their fur. They are house dogs that enjoy our large, fenced-in yard and only visit their "neighborhood friends" when we take them for walks. If we take a multiple-day vacation, our two pampered puppies are boarded at a local professional doggy daycare.

If any single pet is responsible for my transition to being a full-fledged dog lover, it is our puppy, Copper, a purebred Cavalier King Charles Spaniel. He stole my heart from the moment I first saw him. Copper has a digestive problem that requires JoAnne to cook special, large batches of homemade food that agrees with his delicate digestive system. Copper's adopted brother, Benny, a Cavapoo, also benefits from the food. I recognize that someday Copper's time with us will end, and I will be devastated by the loss, but I wouldn't trade the wonderful time and memories we have had together for anything.

Our three house cats, Maggie, Grady, and Sunny, have regular vet visits to maintain their health. Sunny has an illness that requires him to eat special food and take a unique, expensive medication that can only be prepared and purchased at a local compounding pharmacy. All of our pets are more than pets; they are family members. I should also mention that all our pets sleep in bed with us if they choose to. I think it's safe to say I've come a long way since my scarred Skook childhood, and I feel I have been able to get past the many unpleasant animal experiences of my youth and have provided a loving, caring home for our furry friends.

Chapter 5

Ashland seemed to have an overabundance of penny candy stores in the 1960s. Then again, that went hand-in-hand with the flood of Baby Boomer kids that took to the streets daily, and there certainly were a lot of us. Some of these stores were known by just about every kid in town, and others were neighborhood secrets. Some only sold candy, while others sold a few other essential items that most of us kids cared nothing about. Not unlike modern-day drug dealers who hang out on street corners near schoolyards, penny candy stores always seemed to be no more than a stone's throw away from every school building in town.

"Come here, little boy, I have just what you need."

As if getting unsuspecting sugar addicts high on sucrose wasn't evil enough, some stores featured penny gumball machines with special colored gumballs that could be traded for money. I can't recall all the color combinations or their values, but it went something like this. If you scored a green and white striped ball, it might be worth two cents. A red and white might be a nickel, and a solid silver might be worth a dime. I recall seeing gold balls in the machines, but I never knew any kid who got one and can't recall its value.

The logic behind this kiddy gambling was exactly the same as the psychology of casino gambling for adults. The kids would see the prize-winning balls pressed against the front of the gumball machine's rectangular glass dome and spend all their precious pennies with the futile hopes of making the big score. Every once in a while, some kid would score a nickel ball, or maybe a three-center, and all the kids hanging around would go wild. They didn't seem to take into account that to win that nickel gumball, little Johnny dropped about $1.75 of the money he made cutting grass, delivering papers, and turning in soda bottles for pennies.

Granted, little Johnny also had a pocket full of chewable gumballs with enough sugar to send the entire fourth grade into sugar shock or the local dentists into screams of ecstasy at the potential future business. Now that I think about it, maybe the dentists were financing the gumball gambling. This went on at many of the candy stores. I don't know if anyone's parents were aware of this, but I suspect enforcement of the unspoken yet sacred and understood kid code managed to keep this away from the folks since the machines never seemed to go away.

Another weird thing was that many of these corner stores were run by innocent-looking, sweet little old ladies. Some people might say these ladies were simply supplementing their income with a bit of cash, but I think it might have been more sinister than that. When you combine the granny factor with the gambling gumball machines, we may have been dealing with an underworld network of Ma Barkers.

34

We always figured these many stores operated independently, but we might have been wrong. Maybe they were all part of an evil South American sucrose cartel. It was probably the dreaded El Diente Dulce Cartel (Sweet Tooth Cartel). They are known worldwide for flooding countries with sucrose. Okay, so maybe I made that up. All I know is that for us, candy stores were like cheese factories to rats. If they had set mouse traps in the candy aisle, we'd all be missing fingers and toes.

These penny candy stores were like Heaven on Earth. There was no need for us to talk about or even imagine sugar-free treats. Everything sold in those stores was the equivalent of mainlining high-test sugar straight into your veins. It was a sugar junkie's paradise, with every sweet morsel imaginable right there at our fingertips. These were the same types of candy you now pay a fortune for at quaint and nostalgic candy stores you find in most of those cute little towns that have become meccas/tourist traps for unsuspecting travelers.

Remember candy cigarettes? There were two varieties. One type was solid sugar sticks that were shorter and thinner than actual cigarettes. These were sold in small, fake cardboard packs meant to look like national brands. They might have cost a nickel a pack and had, I believe, five candies to a pack. They had a splotch of red dye on the tip to resemble fire. No one would ever mistake these little gems for cigarettes, but we didn't care. Who needs a jolt of nicotine when you can have a super sugar rush?

The second type was a cigarette-shaped bubblegum wrapped in paper that resembled actual cigarettes. The coolest thing about these was some sort of powder, maybe powdered sugar, between the paper and the gum to keep the paper from sticking. If you put one end of the gum cigarette in your mouth and blew, the powder would puff out the front and look like smoke. We would stand on the street corner like wannabe James Deans pretending to puff away and blow powdered sugar smoke from our bubble gum ciggies. It was especially fun in the winter when you could blow out steam that we thought looked even

35

more like smoke. For the record, this pretend game never encouraged me to be a smoker, as I have never smoked in my life.

There was a general five-and-dime store on Centre Street called the Gay Store, named after the owner's daughter, Gay. As a side note, this was a time when "gay" meant happy and had no reference to one's sexual orientation. For us growing up, the name Gay Store meant nothing more than a great five-and-dime store, but as adults, when we spoke about it to people not from the area, it always got a laugh or at least a few raised eyebrows. In addition to having all sorts of things for the home and an excellent cheap toy section, the Gay Store had a great candy counter.

My favorite thing at the Gay Store candy counter was the teaberry-flavored nonpareil container. You could buy these delicious tiny red beads by the ounce, so you could buy as many or as few as you could afford. If I had an extra quarter or fifty cents, I'd head straight to the Gay Store and get some of those luscious goodies. The clerk would measure them out and place them in a small, white candy bag. After that, it would be teaberry-flavored, pure sugar rush ecstasy. There was another store a few blocks away on Centre Street called the Paper Mart. I'm not sure why it was called that, other than maybe they sold paper products in the back part of the store. I never would have known that because I never made it any further than the candy counter at the front of the store. Like every other candy store in town, this one was stocked with all our favorite penny candy, from wax soda bottles filled with sweet juice to flying saucer-shaped wafer morsels containing candy beads.

My favorite thing at the Paper Mart was the small clear toy candies they had every year around Christmas. These incredible hard candies were translucent toy-shaped yellow, red, and green yummies that were pure Heaven to the sweet tooth. The nice thing about them was they were small, fit easily in your mouth, were cheap, and lasted a long time. Many of my fondest memories of "growin' up Skook" were spent in these temples of sweetness known as penny candy stores.

Chapter 6

Candy stores may have been one source of gambling inspiration for us Skook kids, but we had another centered around trading cards. It was one of those things that started out simple but got bogged down with an avalanche of rules very quickly. I'll get into that shortly. But first, let's discuss the phenomenon of trading cards.

Every boy I knew had his own collection of trading cards. We all spent what little money we had on cards, primarily for the cards and secondarily, but no less importantly, for the bubblegum. Remember, this was when cards were cheap, and none of us kids had any idea that one or more of the five cards we got in our nickel pack might someday, a few decades later, be worth a small fortune to some collector. Care was not often taken to protect them. There were no plastic binder sheets to store your collection; if there were, we couldn't have afforded them. My collection was kept in an old shoebox.

We only cared about the cards with pictures and statistics of our favorite baseball stars, which were cool. We even got checklist cards to keep track of our collections, although only the most anal-retentive kids bothered with those. Most of the time, we relied on memory or ruffled through our stack to see which cards we wanted to trade. Do you remember going through your collection to see what cards you had and which you needed? Remember saying, "Got 'em, got 'em, need 'em"? Trading cards with your pals was a great way to build your collection because it didn't take long for you to get doubles or triples, especially of the least famous players. To save time, we sometimes kept our spare cards in a separate stack with a rubber band around them, ready for trading.

And the gum was delicious. I believe it might have been the Topps company that had the best gum. It was almost as big as the cards, was light pink, was covered in powdered sugar, and was soft and flavorful. If I think back, I can still smell and taste that gum in my memory like I was still there. The cards held onto that wonderful smell for quite a while, too. There was another company in the trading card business as well called Fleer. I can't recall for certain, but their gum might not have been as good as the stuff in Topps cards.

I don't know if any of my friends had a complete set of baseball cards, but I doubt it, even with trading. All of us had plenty of duplicates, triplicates, and more. Also, there were other trading cards besides baseball cards. There were football cards and Beatles trading cards during the high point of their fame.

There were also Batman cards with scenes from that hit show during its short TV run. Whenever it was time for the Batman show, I would sit on the floor in front of the TV with my legs crossed and my Batman cards spread out before me. At the time, I was too young and dumb to realize that much of the Batman show was campy and tongue-in-cheek. I just thought it was cool. I'm sure there were many other types of trading cards, but you get the basic idea.

So, you might wonder where gambling fits into all this. I have no idea where this might have originated, but we had a game called "Shooting Cards." Everyone in town knew about it and how to play it. This game could be played inside someone's house or outside. The key was finding the best location. Most games were played outside since we instinctively knew our parents wouldn't approve. My brother and I would practice inside, but we kept the game looking innocent for our parents. There were a handful of standard "known" rules to shooting cards, plus a bunch of other regulations that flexed depending on who was playing the game that day (these were usually attempted by cheaters). Let's look at the simplest form of shooting cards.

Assume you had a stack of one hundred duplicate baseball cards; in other words, you "got 'em, got 'em, but don't need 'em." Now assume your buddy is in the same situation but with some cards different from those you bring. Logically, one would suggest that you could trade with him; that would be the civilized thing to do. It would be a win-win for both of you. But what fun is that? Wouldn't it be better to keep all the cards you don't even care about and take all his cards as well? That was kid logic at its finest. This is where Shooting Cards comes into play.

You choose a wall with a flat, clean, perpendicular surface below. You also determine and mark a foul line that no one's legs can cross, maybe five feet back from the wall. It's also good at this point to establish "leanzies" or "no leanzies," meaning you can lean your arms and top half of your body over the line as long as your feet stay behind the line. This is often critical if your opponent is a knuckle-dragger with monkey arms. As you will see, those simian appendages could give him an unwanted advantage if you allow a "leanzie" situation.

To get the game rolling we would usually flip a coin to see who goes first. Let's assume you lost the toss and have to go first. You take a card from your stack, pinch it between your thumb and index finger, and throw it toward the wall like a mini Frisbee where it bounces off the wall and settles onto the ground. Now it's the other guy's turn. Let's say he does the same thing, and his card lands a few inches from yours. It's your turn again. This back-and-forth process continues until one of your cards covers part of another. When it does, you get to scoop up the entire "pot" of cards. This covering of the card is often called "coverzies."

I should note that before starting the game, you both have to agree on a few rules, like what constitutes "coverzies." Every trading card has a border around the center picture. Common rules say that if your card overlaps the border and touches the picture, that's considered a cover; however, some people modify the rules to say one-third or half of the card must be covered. It's imperative to establish these rules up front to prevent the loss of teeth during the physical altercation that's sure to ensue. This is especially critical when five or six kids are all playing in the same game.

Another thing you need to establish is what kinds of cards are accepted into the game. You may expect a game made up of only baseball cards, but somebody might try to slip in a few Beatles or Man

From U.N.C.L.E. cards. If you don't care about Napoleon Solo or Illya Kuryakin and don't want that to be a problem, you should be certain to establish that criterion upfront.

Also, if you're playing against someone whose morals might be suspect, you should watch out for dummy cards or filler cards. For example, if somebody has an old, incomplete deck of playing cards they don't want, sometimes they will try to sneak those in with legitimate trading cards. That's a major no-no guaranteed to start a shouting match and eventually a brawl. Some really desperate shooters have been known to cut up old pieces of cardboard into trading card size and try to pass them off as the real thing. Usually, the crudely drawn cartoon of a baseball player is a dead giveaway.

That's the most simple version of the game; two or more people shooting against a wall with the covering card taking the spoils. There's another version of the game called "knockzies." That's when you forget about any cards covering other cards. You stand maybe ten cards up against the wall at a slight angle. If two people are shooting, each player contributes five cards. The goal is to take turns trying to knock down the standing cards. Because many shots result in misses, the pot can grow quickly. Whoever knocks down the final card gets the entire pot.

This version of the game led to the creation of what are called "waxies." All the local penny candy stores sold wax soda bottles and wax straws filled with different colors of sweet liquid. This meant every kid had access to all the wax he needed. To make a waxie, you take a regular trading card, and using the empty wax container like a crayon, you rub it back and forth, coating the front and back of the card with wax. This made the card stiffer and heavier than a traditional card. This gave more control of the card when playing "coverzies" and a lot better results when playing "knockzies." Think about a lightweight, flimsy trading card versus a stiff, heavy one.

Another version of Shooting Cards was called "knockzies."

There were several cheat versions of "waxies" that you had to be on alert for. Both were obvious. One type was when some kid would use his wax crayons to modify his card. Although the principle was the same as clear "waxies," the problem was you could no longer tell what the picture on the card was because of the colored scribbles coating the card. The other thing you had to watch for was kids who applied so much wax to their cards that the cards were as thick as a hunk of wood. Ok, maybe not quite that thick, but at least five times heavier than a lightly coated "waxie." The problem with these was the unfair advantage this gave the player during "knockzies."

This is where things got complicated. Technically, all "waxies" should not have been allowed, as they violated the original integrity of the card. But once you agreed to let "waxies" into the game, you had to monitor everyone's turn to ensure they weren't trying to toss a wax two-by-four at the "knockzie" card. So much of this became a judgment call that arguments and fights could break out at any time, especially when four or more kids were playing, and the pot became huge.

It was not uncommon to see a kid show up with a stack of a couple hundred cards and go home empty-handed while the other players split his losses. At the time, we didn't think of this as gambling, any more than we thought of the prize gum balls at the candy stores as gambling, but a rose by any other name ... yadda, yadda, yadda. For us, shooting cards was just another rite of passage, just another part of "growin' up Skook."

Chapter 7

No Skook summer would have been complete without at least one trip to Knobles Grove Amusement Park. (For the record, it's pronounced Kuh-no-bels, not Nobles.) Although located in Elysburg, Columbia County, Knobles was and still is a staple among Skooks and is only about a half hour Northwest of Ashland.

According to the Knobles website history section, in 1828, Reverend Henry Hartman Knoble purchased a parcel of land known as Penny's Farm for $931 and began the family lumber business. In 1880, the family moved to the farm, which became Knobles Grove. The initial park opened on July 4th, 1926, with food stands, a swimming pool, and a merry-go-round. In 1943, the park temporarily closed for World War II. The park continued to grow through the years and experienced major flooding in 1972 from tropical storm Agnes. In 1981, the park changed its name to Knobles Amusement Resort. In 2006, they experienced another flood, with 90 percent of the park underwater. In ten days, it was 90 percent back in operation.

To this day, no matter where I am, every time I smell fresh caramel popcorn, I'm magically transported back to the 1960s and Knobles. This was the era of Knobles I remember best. In my mind, I find myself surrounded by the many luscious aromas there, such as cotton candy, candy apples, and caramel popcorn. (Pronounced "karmul" popcorn in Skook speak.) Although I haven't been to the park in several decades, I still think about returning for a visit every summer, but I have yet to get there, perhaps this year. I must admit, at my age, I am less motivated by the rides than I am by potato pancakes, known in the Skook as bleenies.

My most fond memories of the park are from a time when it was much smaller and a lot less busy. This was before expanded parking areas with trams to transport you to the park and before "pay one price" when you bought a book of tickets and paid per ride.

Several roller coasters and thrill rides have been added over the years. The coaster I remember best is the High-Speed Thrill Coaster that was added in 1955 but would be considered calm, perhaps even a kiddy coaster by today's standards. I hope the number of trees in the park hasn't changed much. I recall the shade these many trees provided on hot summer days. So many amusement parks subject you to unwanted sunlight. If there's one thing besides food I remember about Knobles, it's the shade trees.

When I was little, there was a ride in the kiddy section that was a large brontosaurus. As I recall, it rocked slowly back and forth, and you could spin in a round seat. I assume that ride might not be there any longer, but it was a thrill ride for me as a little kid. This wasn't because it was fast, dangerous, or exciting. It was because, in my creative little mind, I imagined the dinosaur coming to life and eating me. Little did I know that a brontosaurus was an herbivore, and even if it was alive, it would have no interest in taste-testing some dumb little Skook kid.

Our church occasionally had covered dish picnics at Knobles in their pavilions across from the park entrance. Since this was before the park's expansion, my dad could park our car next to the pavilions, and we could simply cross the street to ride the rides. My grandmother, Lucy Metzinger, would sometimes join us at the park, but her interests differed from ours. Gram liked to spend hours in the bingo pavilion and often won some cool prizes. Once, she won a giant purple stuffed poodle and gave it to my siblings and me. We called the thing Fifi since we decided it was a female and a French poodle. We had fun with that toy for many years.

I always enjoyed the carousel merry-go-round at Knobles. If you chose to ride on the outermost horses you would have an opportunity to grab several rings from a mechanical arm during your ride. If I remember correctly, you might have gotten a free ride if you snagged a brass ring. Then, when the ride was just about complete, you could throw the rings back into the collection area. I'd be willing

44

to bet most kids were like me and threw all the rings back, all except one, which I took home as a souvenir.

When I was in high school, our rock band, Isaac, got to play a concert in Knobles' Bandshell, which was pretty cool. Knobles also has a huge swimming pool, but I only swam there once as an adult. They are also known for their campsites, although, not being a camper, I have never used these facilities. In 1973, Knobles built a haunted mansion ride reminiscent of the spook houses of earlier amusement parks. Over the years, Knobles has grown, evolved, and changed with the times, but for me, it remains a proud part of my Skook heritage.

Chapter 8

It was not all fun and games growing up in the Skook. We had more than our share of hoodlums and psychopaths who would take pleasure in beating you for no apparent reason. They roamed the town like jackals, usually in pairs, looking for victims to assault, which somehow they managed to do without prosecution. We all knew their names and their faces and avoided them at all costs.

The police knew them as well since, usually, they were the second or third generation of psychos, having parents or grandparents who were equally insane; however, there was little the cops could do unless they caught these scoundrels in the act. For example, there was one character in town who everyone, including the cops, knew had been setting fires in people's garages. He had come from a long line of firebugs, including one member of his family who was in jail for burning down a local business. But he was out roaming free, setting fires, because he hadn't been caught in the act. I'm unsure what happened to him or if he was ever caught.

Other crazies, prone more to violence than pyromania, were like hyenas hiding in the bushes, waiting for prey. These lunatics appeared out of thin air when you least expected them. You might be minding your own business sitting on a swing at one of the local parks, and they would show up and pounce on you. Not being a very large or strong kid, I became proficient at avoiding these laughing maniacs whenever possible. Being invisible is another of my superpowers. Maybe the term isn't so much being invisible as it is blending into my surroundings so completely and appearing so irrelevant that I'm ignored. This skill has followed me into adulthood to the point where I can stand at a bar with cash in my hand, and bartenders don't even see me.

One evening, my friend Dave and I were walking down Centre Street. We had just passed the Marko Town House and were in front of the liquor store when two local older teenage lunatics walked toward us. I was only about ten or eleven, so I kept my head down and avoided eye contact. I felt something slap my left ear and realized one of them had hit me. I just kept walking and did my best to ignore the sharp pain. These guys were a lot older and bigger than me, and if their reputation was accurate, they were mentally deranged.

When we got to the corner of South Eight Street by what was then Heinz Pharmacy, we turned to the left to head home. We only walked a few feet when the same two lunatics came out of the alley. I thought they were going to kill me, and I didn't have any idea why. I knew their names and knew they were out of school, but they didn't know me. Then I realized they knew Dave or, more importantly, his older brother, Eddie. They didn't like Eddie and apparently decided to vent their frustrations on Dave. They smacked Dave around a bit, left me alone for whatever reason, and then Dave and I ran to our respective homes.

I walked into my house, doing my best to avoid speaking with anyone, as I was sure I might burst out crying if I did. My dad was there with his friend, Bud, a local tough guy who came from a family of tough guys. Bud often helped my dad with local carpentry projects Dad got when he was between jobs. Dad noticed my ear was red and asked what had happened. I, of course, started crying and told him what had happened.

Back then, I wore what we called a "Rocky Belt," which was a thick leather belt with a large square buckle that we wore off to the right side because we thought it made us look cool. Bud pointed to the belt and said, "Next time somebody does something like that to you, take off your belt, swing it, and beat their face with the buckle. If you get a chance, wrap it around their necks and choke them until they pass out." I suppose that would have been good advice for someone more aggressive than I was, but I was more fond of the "run and hide" approach.

48

My dad asked if I knew who these guys were, and I said I did. He and Bud took me out and put me in the back of our car. We drove around looking for them. We found them standing by a light pole near the *Evening Herald* newspaper office, and Dad pulled over. He and Bud got out, grabbed them, and started working them over. I was terrified that Dad or Bud might ask me to join in. As I said, I wasn't the aggressive type, and just being there made me sick to my stomach. The one guy who hit me in the ear kept crying and shouting, "Don't hit me, I'm retarded." Apparently, Bud didn't care what his mental status might be. For the record, those two never bothered me again.

We also had our share of crazies who were not violent and, for the most part, kept to themselves. One was an old gentleman known as "The Prophet." He roamed around town in a dirty white robe with unwashed shoulder-length hair and a thick, matted beard. To the best of my knowledge, he never did anything to hurt or bother anyone. One day, a few friends and I saw him at one of the parks and decided to speak to him.

He was filthy, dirty, and had that smell of the unwashed; once you smell it, you will never forget it for as long as you live. As we talked to him, I saw a large spider walking up his beard, and I said, "A spider is walking up your beard. Should I kill it?"

He replied, "No need to do that; he's not hurting anyone. Just let him be."

Someone else asked him if he could heal sick people. I suppose they figured with the hair and robe, maybe he was like Jesus or had mystical powers. The Prophet replied that he had been able to heal people on occasion. I only half heard the conversation. I was fascinated watching that huge spider walk up his beard and across his face.

Another boy asked, "What would you do to cure someone who had measles?"

The Prophet thought for a moment, then said, "I would remove his foreskin."

49

The Prophet wore a dirty white robe, and he had unwashed, shoulder-length hair, and a thick, matted beard.

I had no idea what a foreskin was and said, "His forehead skin? Why would you remove his forehead skin?"

He corrected me and repeated, "Foreskin." Then he gave me a look that was so creepy I decided it was time to beat feet and get out of there as quickly as possible, which I did. Years later, when I eventually learned what a foreskin was, I realized just how bizarre that old coot was.

We had another guy who was what locals called "slow." He was a tall, thin fellow who was constantly smiling. He would go to the Roxy Theater and sit in the back row; although that wasn't a big deal, the story behind it was interesting. He never paid for a movie as the theater owner knew him and felt bad for him, and the guy would stay in the theater and watch the second showing of the film. If the movie ran all week, he would be there for every show, sitting in the back row and enjoying it as if it were the first time he saw it. Perhaps for him, it was.

Then, there was the nice lady who walked every day along the highway from Locust Dale to Ashland to attend viewings at the local funeral parlors. She could be seen walking the road with her feathered hat and funeral dress. She showed up at every viewing and cried for every deceased person, whether she knew them or not. I always wondered if, when she died, did she have many people to cry for her?

We also had a bit of a wild woman who dressed and combed her hair like a man. Maybe she was a lesbian or transgender, but we kids had no idea what either of those were back then. But we knew she was different. She lived in a rundown house with dozens of wild dogs roaming uncontrolled around her property. Every kid knew to avoid that house, not because of the woman but because of those dogs. She had a brother they called "Tex," who wore cowboy clothes and a cowboy hat.

While "growin' up Skook" may not have always been a good time, it certainly could be interesting. We had our share of tough guys, crazy people, and those you knew to avoid. This proved to be a good lesson for adulthood. To this day, I study people in public situations and look at their eyes for signs of craziness that I know far too well how to recognize.

Chapter 9

In the Skook, back when I was a kid, many things were bought from people who sold their wares door-to-door. Everyone knew of the Fuller Brush Man who came to your house to demonstrate and sell various household items. The man would sit on your sofa in your parlor and pull multiple objects from his leather sample case. They were typically household items he thought you might like to buy. I never realized there was even a brush company called Fuller or that the salesman worked for them. I thought he was the Fulla Brush Man because he had a case fulla' brushes. What did I know about such things? I was just some dumb kid.

We also had the Avon Lady who had all sorts of soaps, shampoos, and bubble baths that Mom would occasionally buy. I never actually saw any Avon Lady, but I knew she came by our house, perhaps when I was at school or outside playing. Every Christmas, I looked forward to some cool Avon products. My brother George and I once got bubble bath liquid in containers that looked like recovered Gemini space capsules. The cool thing about them was that they could be used as banks with combination locks once they were emptied. I can still remember the smell of Avon bubble bath as if I were holding an open bottle under my nose at this moment.

Once, we got soap on a rope, which I thought was the coolest thing around. That soap's fragrance is another smell I can bring to mind instantly. Mom also got us cologne from Avon when we got a little older. I recall the one we got came in a brown glass container shaped like an antique car. I kept that on my dresser between my Aroara Universal Monster models and Big Daddy Roth weirdo creature models, such as Rat Fink, Digger, and others. Those models usually had huge, muscular, bulgy-eyed monsters sticking out the roofs of the suped-up cars. I loved drawing these characters and still use a few of the techniques I stole from these illustrators in my own cartooning today.

We also had the Charles Chip Man, whom we kids called "Charlie Chip." They brought you potato chips or whatever snack you chose to your house in a large metal tin can. If I recall correctly, you paid a deposit on the can, which allowed you to swap an empty can for a full one and only pay for the chips. Those were good chips, as I recall, and environmentally ahead of their time with the reusable tins. I don't know if a man named Charles owned the company, but as far as we were concerned, anyone who brought the can was considered Charlie Chip to us. I recently saw that the company's still in business and using the same returnable cans. I'm unsure who owns the company now, but it wouldn't matter to Skook kids. Whoever brings the can will automatically become Charlie Chip. It's just one of those unwritten Skook rules.

Speaking of environmentally thoughtful, when we bought soda, it came in returnable glass bottles. The deposit was included in the initial price, and when you returned the bottle to the store, you got your deposit back. All of us Skook kids loved finding empty discarded bottles that we could return for a nickel. My friend Ronny's mom often asked him to return a bunch of bottles to the store. There were frequently more bottles than he could carry. He would ask me in Skook speak, "Do ya wanna buddy me ta da A 'n P ta return a buncha bot-als? I'll split it witcha."

I knew what that meant from past experience — a fifty-fifty split of all returns from deposits. I'd do a quick mental calculation based on how many bottles he had and instantly estimate my commission. I may not have been a wiz at math when I was a kid, but I was a walking calculator when it came to figuring out how much money I might make returning bottles; although, back in Schuylkill County in the early 1960s, we couldn't even imagine what a calculator might be, let alone a computer, cell phone, or all the other amazing technologies our kids and grandkids take for granted.

Ronny never disappointed me, either. He was always good for the promised fifty-fifty split. He took that rule to the extreme sometimes. Once, after we had collected our deposits, he ended up with an uneven number of pennies. I figured the extra penny should go to him since these were his bottles. But Ronny didn't agree. Instead, he threw the extra penny far away into some bushes and tall grass. I thought he was nuts. Maybe it was because he was an only child, and money didn't mean much to him. But for me, it was like he had thrown away a gold doubloon.

Whenever he did something like that, I would do my best to remain aloof and act like I completely agreed with him. A stupid penny? No big deal. But as soon as I found myself alone later in the day, I would dive head first into those bushes, looking for that penny. Sadly, I usually was unable to find the treasured one-cent piece. But I'd be lying if I said it didn't affect me. To this day, if I see a coin, even a penny, lying on the ground, I pick it up. This can often be challenging at my age, but I never pass one by. I consider it a rewarding form of exercise.

Another friend of mine once shoplifted a Matchbox police car from a store in town called Shillings. To me, any Matchbox car was like finding the Holy Grail because I couldn't afford them except on rare occasions when I had extra money, like after a birthday. My friend didn't even want the car and seemed to miss the irony of shoplifting a police car. As I recall, he took the vehicle from the box and threw it down the outdoor basement steps of a nearby church. Yes, I also appreciate the irony of stealing something and throwing it down church steps.

I wanted that Matchbox more than anything in the world but I didn't want my friend to know that. I ignored the whole thing, and we headed back to our neighborhood. The next day, however, I hightailed it to that church, ran down the stairs, and scarfed up that Matchbox police car. It was a bit scratched up, and the plastic dome light was broken, but I didn't care. I didn't consider taking the car as stealing because my friend threw it away. Also, he stole it without my knowing about it until we were blocks from the store. He didn't want it and tossed it down the cement stairs. So, technically, this was more like a salvage operation. I'd seen TV shows where companies invest money to salvage sunken ships, hoping to find treasure. I felt this was like that, and it's the defense I plan on presenting someday at the Pearly Gates.

I considered this more like a salvage operation.

We also had many other products sold door to door, such as Girl Scout cookies. Every year, one of the local Girl Scouts would knock on our door, selling a variety of yummy delights. My favorites were shortbread cookies, which were much different than the bland versions of the cookies sold today. These babies were twice as sweet even before the company coated them with pure cane sugar. Then, they became the greatest shortbread cookies on Earth.

We had farmers who drove through the neighborhood selling their wares, shouting out the different fruits or vegetables they had to offer. Also, there was the ever-popular Mr. Softy, whose ice cream truck roamed the streets playing that annoying jingle that brought kids streaming from their homes in search of icy delights. I can't imagine listening to that wretched tune all day long without going crazy.

We also had a rag man who drove around the neighborhood paying money for rags, clothes, metal, etc. We called him "the sheeny" because that was what the adults called him. It wasn't until my adulthood that I learned that the term "sheeny" was a derogatory insult toward a Jewish person. As a kid, I never knew anyone who was Jewish. This was just one of the many offensive terms we used regularly to refer to certain races or nationalities of people. We were kids, and while learning, we spoke as we were taught. As a somewhat enlightened adult, I have done my best to put those negative common 1960s Skook words behind me.

Kids were also always selling stuff for school door-to-door. I remember selling flower seeds in the spring for some school fundraiser. I have no idea why we were selling them; I just did what I was told. The seeds came with a catalog that showed all sorts of incredible gifts you could get from selling these packets of future plants. I couldn't imagine at the time how difficult it would be to get any of these prizes, but I daydreamed of the riches I would get from my impromptu seed business. Unfortunately, I learned through these exercises in futility that I would make an abysmal salesman. Here is an example of one of my typical sales encounters. Imagine me standing in front of the home. I ring a doorbell, and an older lady with white hair answers the door.

Lady: "Hello, young man. What can I do for you today?"
Me: "Uh … um … I'm… sellin' seeds fer school."

Lady: "Oh, I see. Is this for a fundraising project?"

Me: "Uh … yeah … a fundraiser."

Lady: "May I ask what the fundraising project is for?"

Me: "Um … I dunno. The teacher just tolt me ta go out and sell these stupid seeds, so here I am."

Lady: "And you mean to tell me you don't know why you are selling these seeds?"

Me: "Nope. Just 'cause the teacher tolt me to."

Lady: "Don't you think you should care what you are raising money for?"

Me: "Nope."

Lady: "Well. I suppose then I don't need any seeds today."

Me: "Ok, bye."

And off I would go without selling a single pack of seeds and losing all hope of getting any of the amazing prizes. Sadly, my sales technique never improved, and to this day, I probably couldn't sell a glass of ice water to a man in a desert dying of thirst. Hopefully, other door-to-door salespeople had better sales techniques than I did and had more success selling in the Skook.

Chapter 10

For as long as I can recall, my family and I attended the First Presbyterian Church on North Ninth Street in Ashland. I'm not exactly sure why my parents chose that church other than it was only a block from our house. In the 1970s, the Methodist church at the corner of Eleventh and Center Streets merged with the Presbyterian church, and the name was changed to the Methodist-Presbyterian church. But during my childhood, we were Presbyterians, and that's how I was raised and eventually confirmed.

My dad, the son of my Italian immigrant grandfather, Pietro Malafarina, was raised Catholic, like most good Italian boys. I don't know if my German paternal grandmother, Lydia Texter Malafarina, was Catholic. My mom was raised Protestant. I've been told it wasn't an easily accepted thing for a Catholic and a Protestant to marry back when they were young. My dad told me he got kicked out of the Catholic church for marrying my mom. I don't know how accurate that statement might have been as Dad liked to embellish somewhat ... as in a lot.

Apparently, the negative view of my parents marrying went beyond the religious connotations and into the realm of conflicting nationalities. My mom's maiden name was Lois Gertrude Metzinger, and it was about as German-American as you could get. Her mother, my maternal grandmother, was Lucille Magdeburg, and my maternal grandfather was Robert Metzinger. Pass the Wiener schnitzel, please.

My dad's name at birth was Georgio Ernesto Malafarina, but he changed it to George Thomas Malafarina. His family was as Italian-American as pizza. My mom once told me that at the time she married my dad, a Protestant German girl marrying a Catholic Italian boy was looked at by people much like an interracial marriage was in the late 1950s. I don't know if things were as drastic as Mom believed, but I suspect they might have been a bit rough.

Years later, in 1972, I experienced some of what she expressed to me. I was dating a German-Irish Protestant girl whose blue-haired great-aunt was Irish Catholic. And yes, bluing an old lady's hair was a thing back then. When I met the lady, I knew I would be put under the ethnic/religious microscope; however, I suppose I passed her scrutiny because I learned later how she described me to other relatives. She said, "He's Italian ... but he's nice."

Wow. Talk about your left-handed compliments. That one ranked right up there with, "Hey, you don't sweat much for a fat chick." I hated bursting her bubble, but since my paternal grandmother was German, my dad was only half-Italian. Since my Mom was German on both sides, I was hardly Italian at all. I always say that I only ended up with the name and the nose. My sons Mike and Alex carry on the Italian surname, but that's about as much from the tip of the boot-shaped fatherland as they got. Since Mike married a girl of half-Italian descent, Laura, I suppose his son, my grandson, Luca Joseph Malafarina, may have more Italian in him than his father.

Getting back to the Presbyterian church, whatever the reason my folks chose that particular denomination, we kids were required to attend Sunday school and church faithfully every week. My mom wanted to make sure we had a good understanding of all things biblical. I'm not exactly sure if all that education helped me, but I suppose since I've never been arrested and don't have any bodies buried in my backyard, some of it must have gotten through.

I hope my writing horror fiction, where monsters and demonic creatures devour humans and suck their souls, doesn't qualify as a strike against me on the Heavenly tote board. I like to think the opposite. Most times, the antagonists in my stories end up getting their comeuppance. It's not that I try to preach or teach anything in my writing; it's simply that in the fictional world of my stories, I like to stick it to the bad guys when it makes literary sense. Sadly, that is something that truly does distinguish fiction from reality. In the real world, the bad guys win way too often. Sometimes, they even make it to the White House, but that's a saga for another day. Now that I think about it, maybe I did learn something in Sunday school after all.

To support our Sunday School lessons, we received thin printed three- or four-page booklets with that week's lesson spelled out and various stories relating to the lesson. It was printed on shiny paper, and I learned how to have some fun if the lesson got boring, which happened more often than not. I could erase or scratch out some words and letters and replace them with my own. This made for many imagination-stimulating ideas and lots of fun. For example, one lesson story was entitled "Sermon on the Mount." I put my eraser, pencil, and imagination to work to create a baseball story I called "Herman on the Mound." If the story said, "In the beginning ..." I could easily add it to my baseball story and make "in the big inning." It was amazing how easy it was to convert that religious tale into a baseball classic. I don't suppose I'll burn in the eternal flames for that little stunt, but it probably earned me a black mark or two for anyone keeping score.

In the main part of the church, on the left side of the stone arch and next to the pulpit, is something cool. If you stand perpendicular to the stones that make up the arch and look at them head-on, one of them looks remarkably like Christ in profile. That is, at least, like how the various images of Christ have portrayed him. I'm unsure if everyone can see it or if it is only visible to those of us with an overactive imagination or right-brained creativity. I was able to see it clearly, and when I was in high school, I made a sketch of it. I don't recall whatever happened to that sketch. Maybe someday I'll go back and do another. For the record, I don't believe it's some sort of miracle or any such thing, but it's just one of those cool, weird, coincidental things.

As part of our religious requirements, my brother and I had to say our prayers every night before bed. It wasn't necessarily something we wanted or felt inspired to do, but it was something Mom insisted we do. We figured it was just one of those things, like going to Sunday school every Sunday morning and then to church right after

Sunday school. If Mom wanted us to say our prayers, we would certainly do so.

When we were little, our bedtime prayer was not the typical "Now I lay me down to sleep" prayer. That came later when we were a bit older. I suspect Mom might have realized we (especially me) might freak out at the part that went, "If I should die before I wake." Even at a young age, I was not a big fan of dealing with death, especially my own. You must admit that particular prayer is a bit heavy for a little kid to handle. "What do you mean if I should die before I wake? I'm just a kid! I don't want to talk about dying!"

I knew about the prayer and could have recited it if I was inclined to, but I preferred to skip all that death talk for as long as possible. One of the older neighborhood boys who knew the prayer also knew another somewhat sacrilegious version of the prayer that he would recite to make everyone laugh. It went, "Now I lay me down to sleep, a bag of peanuts at my feet. If I should die before I wake, I leave them to my Uncle Jake."

That was one of those funny things you enjoyed and laughed at but did so while looking around to make sure God didn't notice you laughing. You didn't want to get too many of those black checkmarks. There was another ditty that a Catholic kid in school taught me. It went, "Hail Mary, full of grace, forty chickens in a race." I have a feeling that one might be worse than that peanut thing when it comes to catching the express train to Hell.

Anyway, I didn't use the "Now I lay me down to sleep" prayer until I felt I was old enough to talk to God about dying in my sleep or just felt too old to be reciting the kiddy prayer my mom taught us to say. That kiddy prayer went like this, "Six little angels around my bed. Two to watch, two to pray, two to keep sickness away." That was followed by the mandatory "God bless" list, where we ran down the list of family members we wanted God to bless. This also would include any relatives "up in Heaven."

62

I always felt we could have cut those dearly departed folks from the list to save time and streamline the prayer process; I am not trying to be petty, just logical. After all, if they were already up in Heaven, they were supposedly already blessed. If they were in the other place, then a blessing from me would be a moot point. Besides, what good would any prayer request from some dumb earthly kid do? I wasn't special, and to the best of my knowledge, I didn't possess any heavenly power that might allow me to request special treatment for those cloud-based relatives of mine. This is especially true when you consider that same kid was simply repeating a chant he had been forced to memorize and recite night after night under threat of eternal damnation. Worse than that, not doing so might break my mother's heart. Good boys didn't break their mothers' hearts. It just wasn't done.

So every night we did the prayer and God bless thing. Somewhere along the line, my brother and I realized that if we started saying our prayers while simultaneously pulling our bed covers down, we could shave a few seconds off our prayer responsibilities. We tried it, and it seemed to get the ritual done quicker. By the time we were in bed, we were past the poem part and well into the God blesses. Sweet!

Then we realized that if we started saying our prayers silently once we got to the top of our stairs, we could be almost done by the time we got down the hall, into our room, and under the covers. You guessed it, that worked great as well. Soon, this new ritual also evolved, as such things always seem to do, and became a contest to see which of us would finish our prayers first. Before long, we were saying our prayers as we headed up the stairs. Then not only that, but we were saying our prayers as quickly as possible in our competition to outdo each other. Isn't sibling rivalry a great thing? We raced down our upstairs hall, our unintelligible prayers sounding less like a sacrament and more like a sacrilege. If God was listening to our prayer competition, he might have been able to pick out a few intelligible words among those dual buzz saw sounds posing as a religious declaration.

    I don't recall how far we let the insanity progress or why we eventually stopped and went back to prayers at normal speed, but I suspect my mom may have caught wind of our activities and put her foot down. That was the end of the prayer competition.

    My dad used to help at the church with things like cutting the grass, shoveling snow, trimming the short hedge surrounding the front of the property, and other similar tasks. That meant my younger brother, George, and I often got roped into helping. I hated cleaning debris out from the base of the hedge. It was a dry, dusty, and prickly business. Since the high school was only a block away, lots of litter like cigarette butts, matches, and empty cigarette packs found their way into the hedge, and I had to clean that nonsense out as well. I was also no fan of cutting the grass in the summer or shoveling snow in the winter; however, good boys do what they are told. Being a good boy, I did what was asked of me.

One thing about our church always freaked me out big time, particularly when I was alone. That was the church basement. It had a coldness that, although refreshing on hot summer days, brought a damp mustiness that always made me uncomfortable. If I think back, I can imagine that precise smell all these years later. My footsteps echoed on the concrete flooring, and occasionally, one or more of the bare hanging incandescent light bulbs might go out. That basement terrified me, and to this day, it is often the scene of many of my most frightening nightmares. I know how ridiculous that sounds. Why would anyone be afraid of any part of a church? It's God's house, right? Or I should say God's basement? But it nonetheless frightened me as a little kid alone in such a vast, spooky place.

One of my other jobs at church was handing out bulletins. My friend Bill and I would stand in the vestibule handing out these eight and a half inch by eleven inch folded guides to the day's service. My mom often typed the blue mimeograph cut sheet for these at home, and then my dad and I would go to the church basement, strap the sheet to the mimeograph machine, add ink to the barrel, load the sheets that were blank on one side and printed with some religious pictures on the other, then run off a bunch of them for me to hand out on Sunday. Usually, my friend Bill and I would fold them Sunday morning before handing them out. Sometimes, other friends would join us and help out.

I got to learn a lot of great and often twisted jokes while waiting for customers to arrive. Bill was two years older than me and was a font of knowledge regarding the notorious "Mommy, Mommy" jokes of the late 1960s. These were always formatted first with a question from a child, followed by the punch line/answer from the mommy telling you to shut up and ... whatever. For example:

"Mommy, Mommy, why is Daddy so green?"
"Shut up and dig."

"Mommy, Mommy, I hate my brother's guts."
"Shut up and eat what's put in front of you."

"Mommy, Mommy, why am I running around in a circle?"
"Shut up, or I'll nail your other foot to the floor."

These were particularly bad jokes when told anywhere, but in the vestibule of our church, while handing out bulletins, they became especially nasty. At least they were funny to some slightly warped kids, unlike some of the old guy jokes that we were forced to endure.

One old codger who thought himself particularly funny told us the same joke every Sunday without fail. He would lean over and whisper conspiratorially, "Do you think the rain will hurt the rhubarb?" Then we would anxiously wait, even though we heard this stupid joke a million times. He would respond, "Not if it's in the can." Then, he would laugh like a lunatic. Now that I think back, I suppose he might have been a bit on the senile side. At least we were able to make him happy for a bit.

I also usually got to help take up the collection. This involved four volunteers who often sat at the back of the church. Sometimes, we sat with our families, which added a few seconds to the process. At the appropriate point in the service, we would meet at the rear of the church in the aisle between the two sets of pews. Next, we would approach the front of the church where our minister would bring a stack of offering plates, one for each of us. Two of us would take the two outside isles and two the inside. We would work our way to the back of the church and wait for the appropriate organ procession to play. Then we would carry our money trays to the front, the minister would relieve us of our bounty, and we'd return to our seats.

There was always some job that needed to be done at our church, and somehow, I always seemed to get roped into volunteering. I remember my mom making dozens of stuffed clowns for the Ladies' Aid bizarre. She also made covered dish goodies for our annual church picnic held at the Higher Ups Park, which is the location of two of Ashland's tourist attractions — the Pioneer Tunnel Coal Mine tour and the Lokie steam train ride. As with most young Skook kids, the church was a large part of our young lives and probably kept us from getting into more severe mischief.

Chapter 11

Oh, technology. Some of you may assume this is where I go off on a tangent about the wonders of modern technology. After all, in the past fifty years, we have seen an incredible technological revolution, which is still continuing. As a retired advanced CAD/CAM (computer aided design/computer aided manufacturing) engineer, I have been honored to ride that technology train. I've been fortunate enough to have worked with CNC (computer numerical control) machine programming, robotics, and almost every sort of automated manufacturing technology you can imagine.

However, I'm sorry to disappoint. The technology I'm going to discuss is much more down-to-earth than that. I'm talking about simpler things that most of my friends and I didn't have in the 1960s. Even though the technology was available, most of us didn't have the money to afford such luxuries.

Let's look first at garden hoses and hose nozzles. If you were fortunate enough to have an outside faucet and were even more financially capable, you might have a garden hose attached to that faucet. Most garden hoses I encountered in my youth had no special nozzle on the front. The water came out of the open end of the hose. That was it. If you wanted to increase the water flow or make it have a certain spray pattern, you had to put your thumb over the open end of the hose and make the water shoot out as you desired. This was an acquired skill that took lots of practice. Plenty of us kids got a good soaking trying to master this technique. I always considered this a plus during the hot summer months.

This is where technology enters the picture. I remember going to one of our neighborhood kid's houses and seeing an actual nozzle on the end of their hose. It was a thin, tapered, brass gadget that could easily be adjusted by turning a circular section of the nozzle. It was nothing like the nozzles we buy today. Today's gadgets have a dial on the front, allowing you to choose from many settings. Interestingly, you can still buy this older type of nozzle today in many hardware stores and home centers. Unlike the newer styles, these older styles could be counted on to last for many years. I generally have to replace my new-fangled plastic nozzle every year.

The thing was, in the early 1960s, encountering one of these brass wonders was incredible. It was akin to showing a Bic lighter to an ancient tribe of lost natives. I could never imagine being able to actually someday own one of these marvels of technology. It would mean my highly developed skill of thumb spraying would become obsolete. Such is the way of technology.

It was the holy grail of hose technology.

Another thing I didn't get to experience until late in the 1960s was color TV. Our television was black and white, as were most of the programs. I remember the first color TV show I ever saw. My friend

Dave's parents had a color TV, and they invited my family to watch the annual showing of The Wizard of Oz. I patiently sat through the black and white portion of the movie, knowing it would soon switch to color. I had to pretend I wasn't scared when Elmira Gulch, played by Margaret Hamilton, came on the scene on her bike with that dreaded song in the background. I had seen the movie in black and white several times before and knew she would eventually reappear as the Wicked Witch of the West. Those flying monkeys were really disturbing.

When Dorothy eventually woke up in the land of Oz, the console TV burst into incredible revolutionary Technicolor's three-strip color. Of course, I didn't know this bit of information then; all I knew was that I was sitting on the floor with my legs crossed and my mouth hanging open in disbelief. For a little kid, that was like having a movie theater in your living room, only smaller. Way back then, I had no idea that someday I'd be watching a huge, flat-screen smart TV in my own house. (And craving an even bigger one.)

We probably finally got our own color TV when I was in my early teens. I know this because we still didn't have one when I was eleven. My oldest sister, Louise, got married when I was eleven, and she and her husband, George Nasados, lived in an apartment above Kitty and Dotty's flower shop a few blocks from my house. I recall I wanted to see a sci-fi movie that was scheduled called First Men In the Moon, but I wanted to watch it in color. My sister had a color TV, so my brother and I went to her place to watch it. Very cool.

Speaking of televisions, our simple black-and-white TV was as basic as possible, with a knob for volume, one for channel selection, and one for adjusting the contrast, whatever that was; however, our TV didn't have a remote. I should clarify that statement. It did have something like a remote, and that was me. I changed the channel on command, which happened often. I became very familiar with the channel selection knob in my capacity as a defacto remote. In fact, I suppose I was one of the first voice-controlled channel changers.

"Tommy, change to channel six." Watta ya know? I was on the cusp of technological advancement back then and didn't even know it.

Another thing we were lacking in our house was an efficient toaster. We had a toaster, but it only had two slice slots. This was typical of all of my friend's families. However, our toaster had to accommodate six people, which could often be a challenge. I once saw a toaster with four slices on some TV show, maybe on My Three Sons, but I always figured only rich people could afford that. So we got by with our two-slicer.

Dishwashers were another luxury we knew little about. When my sisters were still living at home, they, apparently, were all the dishwashers we needed. Come to think of it, they, too, were voice-controlled dishwashers, although they often whined and complained. Eventually, my mom got a portable dishwasher that we stored under the counter and pulled out and connected to the sink faucet whenever she wanted to use it.

I'm sure there were other luxuries and labor-saving devices we didn't have or perhaps didn't even know existed that we consider necessities now. But back then, we always seemed to get by in the Skook.

Chapter 12

When I was just a wee lad of six or seven, I discovered I loved to draw and did so every chance I could. I always leaned toward drawing either cartoons or strange, exotic space weapons. In fourth grade at First Street Elementary School, I recall that my friend Eric and I got in trouble for drawing complex and elaborate space laser guns, then holding our tablets and pretending to shoot each other. Our teacher, Miss Flanagan, was not impressed. I suppose today, in our zero-tolerance world, we would both be sent for mandatory psychological counseling. (It might not have been a bad idea back then, either.)

Whenever I practiced drawing at home, I drew on white five by seven-inch shiny cardboard my mom saved from her and my sisters' pantyhose packages. This was nice, sturdy stock, and, most importantly, free. I would try to copy popular cartoons of the day, taking my time and studying all the lines and curves the cartoonists made. Even at that young age, I realized that every scratch the cartoonist made on the paper defined his style. It was him putting his personality into every stroke of his pen.

This is somewhat hard to explain, but I'll make a feeble attempt. Although I tried to copy every detail as closely as possible, I could never accurately duplicate what I thought of as the essence of the drawing, which was the artist's style. To this day, I still cannot.

For example, if you look at Charlie Brown from Peanuts fame, you might think that duplicating his image would be easy since it is essentially a simple drawing, a circle with a face made up of curves and squiggles. But I quickly learned it was more difficult than one might think. I might draw a good likeness of the character, and although most people would instantly recognize the drawing as Charlie Brown, no one would ever mistake it for a drawing Charles Shultz had created. It would be too tight, too stiff, too deliberate, and wouldn't

73

flow. It lacked something. It lacked Charles Shultz. After a bit, you might think it looked like Charlie Brown as seen in a slightly distorted mirror, or maybe Charlie Brown's somewhat odd-looking twin brother who might have had his head squeezed with forceps during birth.

What these drawings were missing was Charles Schultz's inner feelings and emotions. Then, I realized it was ok to study these various cartoonists' techniques and practice drawing by copying their styles, but I could never completely duplicate what they had done. This was fine with me because I knew I would use these early experimentation years to develop my own style someday. And that was exactly what I did. In the following years, I learned the styles of Don Martin and Sergio Aragones from *Mad Magazine*, Bob Kleeben, Sam Gross, and Gahan Wilson, to name a few. I also tried to mimic the styles of popular commercial artists of the day. One of my favorites in my early teen years was Peter Max. His work was unique, recognizable, and fun to draw.

In seventh grade, I met a fellow student who lived in Fountain Springs, whom I'll call Joe. He was a terrific artist and could draw better than anyone I had met up to that point, myself included. We quickly became friends because of our love of drawing, especially cartoons and technical-style drawings such as houses, guns, cars, etc. I had many great opportunities to study his drawing style in the homeroom and study halls when I was supposed to be studying. Has anyone ever really studied in study halls?

Sadly, I came to school one day, and Joe was no longer there. Our teachers all looked sad and were speaking in hushed tones. Several of the girls in our homeroom were crying. That was when I learned that Joe had been killed that morning, having been accidentally struck by a car along the Fountain Springs highway, Route 61. I was stunned and didn't really know how to deal with this. He was the first friend I ever had that had died. I can no longer recall his sketches, but I can see his face clearly in my mind, and I will always be grateful for the inspiration I received from enjoying his drawings and our short friendship.

By the time I was in eighth grade, I had gained a bit of a reputation for being the "guy who could draw stuff." As I mentioned, I was a big fan of Peter Max, who all my friends and I assumed had done the artwork for the Beatles' Yellow Submarine movie. In later years, I learned that although Peter was a close friend of the Beatles and had done many early Yellow Submarine drawings, he was only used as a consultant in the early stages of the film's development. The animation design of Yellow Submarine uses an art style that greatly resembles his, but the film's art director was, in fact, a man named Heinz Edelmann, who called himself "The German Peter Max." Edelmann was the artist who created the actual artwork and animation for that movie.

I often copied the style of Peter Max when I was a teenager.

I had the opportunity to see Peter Max at an art show he had near Philadelphia around 2010. Seeing him as an old guy leaning against the second-floor railing outside an art gallery in the King of Prussia mall was strange. People walked by and didn't pay any attention to him. No one had any idea that one of the most famous artists of a generation was standing right next to them.

The reason I mention Peter Max and Yellow Submarine was not just because I enjoyed drawing in Peter's style back then, but also because a good friend of mine was a rabid Beatles fan and was obsessed with the movie Yellow Submarine. He asked me if I would do a favor for him. He had a paperback book that summarized the film Yellow Submarine in drawings. They were great color images that, at the time, we thought were done by Peter Max. I had no knowledge of Heinz Edelmann; for all I know, the drawings might have been his. But that didn't matter to me. My friend asked me if I would duplicate the book's drawings on paper for him. In other words, each book page would become a separate drawing on a separate sheet of paper.

I couldn't resist the challenge and I quickly agreed. I can't recall if I ever finished all the book's drawings or only did a few. I also have no idea what happened to those drawings, but I had a great time doing them. The task occupied many of my so-called study halls. I never seemed to find time to study during study halls. That might explain a lot about my grades, which were less than stellar.

Also, in eighth grade, a friend, Keith, showed me something amazing. Magazines and catalogs often use glossy paper. Other than changing those stories in my Sunday School handouts, I never paid much attention to things on that type of paper. Keith showed me how to take a black and white picture from a Sears catalog and, using a pencil eraser, remove part of the picture and then draw in whatever you wanted. Since the photo was black and white, the pencil drawing you added fit in flawlessly.

I probably should mention at this point that my friend was a bit of a pervert, as all of us boys were at that age, and anything that could produce sexual content was considered supreme. For example, Keith showed me how to take a bra ad from the Sears catalog, erase the garments from the models, replace them with a sketch of the real goods, and use shading techniques to make the modified image look as real as possible. Suddenly, study halls made sense to me; however, what we were studying probably wouldn't have gone over well with the teachers or our parents if we were caught.

Every year in October, our junior and senior high students could submit colored drawings for consideration for Halloween window painting. This was a practice started by the high school art teacher, Mrs. Emma Irwin, many years earlier. It was an honor to have your drawing chosen, but the real thrill came from transferring it onto a large storefront window with tempera paints. That was often a tough challenge, depending on the complexity of your artwork. Just because you were able to put your idea to paper didn't mean you could successfully translate the image onto a large storefront window with paints.

Although it was always a challenge, it was also a lot of fun, and you got to have a day away from school. That alone was worth the trouble. You were allowed to paint all day but had to be finished by 4:00 pm. One year, I believe, in eighth grade, I managed to win third place in the window painting contest. That was the only time I won anything, but I didn't care; I still painted every year because it was fun and a Skook tradition that still goes on today.

Chapter 13

"We never guess; we look it up." That was the slogan of an initiative in the 60s known as the Look It Up Club. No, it wasn't a TV show or anything as exciting as that. It was, however, a program presented to my fifth-grade class at the WC Estler Elementary School, which we all called "the Seventeenth Street School." The school was eventually condemned, torn down, and replaced with a Turkey Hill mini-market. The purpose of the Look it Up program was to encourage kids not to believe everything they heard and simply accept so-called facts at face value but to research at the library or, if you owned encyclopedias, look it up. Hence the slogan, "We never guess, we look it up."

In my young opinion, that program was a great idea and one that made perfect sense to me. I was basically an honest kid, and I assumed everyone else was too. Unfortunately, that made me quite gullible, and more often than not, I believed whatever I was told. I never thought of questioning anything someone told me, especially an adult. I would never have considered trying to disprove anything I was told. That was one of the reasons I liked the Look it Up Club. It taught me to always question and never believe everything that might seem slightly off. The lessons learned would serve many people well in these days of fake news, Photoshopped pictures, deepfakes, and social media.

Our family may not have had much, but we were fortunate enough to have a complete set of *Worldbook Encyclopedias*, including the adult and childrens' editions. I don't know how we acquired them, whether my parents bought them from a door-to-door encyclopedia salesman or if they were bought second-hand. Reading and education were extremely important to my mom, so I suspect she was the catalyst behind their purchase.

Long before I ever heard of the Look It Up Club, even when I was just learning to read, I was an avid user of our childrens' encyclopedia. It had many pictures and illustrations to study and imagine what they were all about. If I wasn't sure, I would simply make up a story to accompany the image. Sometimes, my mom would read me some poems and nursery rhymes. Eventually, when I was learning to read, I would start with the rhymes because I had most of them memorized and could pretend I was reading.

But my favorite thing was just sitting and staring at the images, daydreaming, and making up my own stories. Sometimes, I would try to act out what I saw. I remember one illustration of three kids in a washbasket with a makeshift sail comprised of towels attached to a broom handle. They brandished wooden swords and wore folded newspaper pirate hats and a patch over one eye. I thought this picture was the coolest thing on the planet, so much so that after intently studying it for a week or so, I tried to recreate it in my mom's wicker laundry basket. That experiment didn't work out as well as my then five-year-old imagination had hoped, but at least I tried.

One thing I enjoyed that always worked well was when Mom or Dad brought a big empty cardboard box home. I have no idea where these boxes came from or what they originally contained, but for me, they became my personal rocket ships. Whenever I was lucky enough to get one of these beauties, I would grab a couple of my crayon pieces and go to work drawing the gauges and switches that made up the control panel inside the box/spaceship. One stupid empty box could easily become a world of incredible space travel adventures for a young boy with a wild imagination.

You probably noticed that I said crayon pieces and not crayons. Up until I was about six or seven, I had no idea there was such a thing as a whole crayon. We had a metal cookie tin filled with crayon halves and quarters of every color imaginable. Many of them appeared multi-colored from banging into each other inside the cookie tin. Some still had bits of paper attached, some had none, and some had paper that slid around when you tried to use them. On a few of the pieces, some of the color names on the paper were readable, such as "red" or "blue," while others had the paper partially torn off, resulting in colors such as "range," "genta," "ello," "purp" and "viol." For the longest time, I thought that was how crayons came — in pieces — until one Christmas at Sunday school, I was given a ten-pack box of brand new Crayola Crayons. I was shocked to learn that they were actually a few inches long and had a real point shape and not a partially ripped paper end with a weird angle worn on the tip.

At first, I didn't want to use them. They were so perfect, pristine, and amazing to my young eyes. Eventually, I gave in to the temptation and decided to try to color something with them. That was when I learned why we had so many partial crayons. I doubt I was very far into my coloring when the first crayon broke in half. How could that be? I wasn't aggressive in my coloring technique. I was no savage barbarian of the arts. I was not a crayon-wielding Viking setting out to pillage a sheet of paper.

That was when I realized the true reason for the broken crayon. As odd as it might seem, I somehow knew I was on to something. Somewhere in the faraway land of Crayola, where these magnificent multi-colored crayons grew on trees, were picked at harvest time, and placed neatly into boxes, something evil was afoot. The malicious trolls who packaged these freshly picked morsels must have been given orders by the supreme master plucker troll to gently tap each one with a special crayon-denting hammer. This way, every unsuspecting kid that tried to use one would have it immediately broken in half like his or her poor shattered heart at seeing their prize possession snapped in two.

I had no idea at that time that there was no magical Crayola land or that the crayons were made by the Binney and Smith Company in Bethlehem, Pennsylvania, which was only about an hour and a half from where I sat heartbroken on the floor, shattered and staring teary-eyed at my broken crayon. Perhaps I shouldn't have guessed, but I should have looked it up in my encyclopedia.

Malicious trolls dented every crayon with a hammer.

I think this is why many of my generation and I are so fascinated by the Internet and iPhones. It's incredible how virtually any question we need an answer to is instantly available at our fingertips, twenty-four hours a day, seven days a week. In the past, if you were out with friends and someone asked a strange question, usually everyone looked at each other confused and said, "Beats me. I don't know." Or if that person was the type who might spout some ridiculous theory that you suspected was nothing but balonie, you had to wait until you got home to try to find the answer in your trusty

World Book Encyclopedia or, as they used to say on the show Rowan and Martin's Laugh-In, "Look that up in your *Funk and Wagnalls*."

Now, however, when someone blurts out something ridiculous, you simply have to take out your iPhone, tap a few keys, and you can prove them wrong. This is the ultimate realization of "We never guess, we look it up." It is the Look It Up Club on steroids. It makes you the ultimate master of truth and accurate information at all times, assuming you go to the proper internet location.

A bit of warning, however; this ease of access to knowledge may also make you the most friendless correct person on the planet. It appears that some people find it offensive to be questioned or, Heaven forbid, proven wrong. Maybe it's better to know you're right and keep that information to yourself. It's always a good idea to look it up for clarification purposes, but depending on the friend, leaving them with delusions of grandeur might be the more prudent avenue.

Until I wrote the first *Growin' Up Skook* book, if anyone had asked me if I was an avid reader as a child, I probably would have denied it and said that I didn't really start reading for pleasure until after graduating. My original childhood memories involved lots of time spent outdoors playing with friends. I remember seeing monster movies at the Roxy Theater and drinking vanilla cokes at Weymans' restaurant. But once I started looking back and remembering my younger days, I realized that I had spent a good deal of time reading my family's encyclopedias. Like today's internet, the encyclopedia had answers to all the important questions I might want to ask, and I was a curious boy with many questions.

I also enjoyed two things in the adult encyclopedias I only investigated when no one was around. One was found in the "F" encyclopedia and featured a multi-layered image of a frog which allowed you to turn transparent celluloid pages with various anatomical organs printed on them, and as you turned the pages, you removed multiple layers of the frog, essentially dissecting it. Of course, after looking at all the frog's internal guts and stuff, you could simply reverse the process, flip the pages, and reconstruct the frog.

Although that was cool, it wasn't as cool as the "H" volume, which had the same multi-page celluloid feature but was of a human body. I can't recall if it featured a male or female body, but like the frog, it also allowed you to turn pages to see inside the human body. If it was a woman, I'm sure I would have preferred to turn these pages in reverse and stare at the naked lady when no one was around. If it was a nude man, I never cared about that one except for the innards. I believe the reason I can't recall which sex was represented (perhaps both) is that there was a plastic transparent model of the anatomy of a female body for sale at Shilling's store, and we little degenerates enjoyed staring at the cover of the box.

We didn't have a lot of books in our house, but I remember my mom enjoyed *Readers Digest*, although I never bothered reading those. One Christmas, I remember Mom and Dad bought me a set of about ten "classic" paperback books with such greats as *Call of the Wild*, *White Fang*, and several others. I don't recall how many of them I may have read, although I remember reading *Call of the Wild*. That's probably why I always think I never read much when I was small; none of the books impressed me that much.

A book that got my attention and was likely instrumental in making me the horror fiction writer I am today was a book I probably wasn't supposed to see. It was a collection of stories by Edgar Allan Poe. The book belonged to one of my older sisters, either Georgine, who was four years older than me, or, more likely, Louiseann, who was eight years older than me. They would have been twelve and sixteen, respectively, at that time.

I can still recall opening that hardcover book when I was at home alone, knowing it was something I wasn't supposed to do, which made it all the more forbidden and exciting. To this day, I can still smell the musty fragrance of the old and worn book. I had always had a love/hate relationship with the horror genre. I loved the Aurora company Universal Monster models, scary movies, and monster magazines, but I also slept with a night light and the covers pulled over my head at night, believing that thin sheet of fabric would protect me from all evil. I had read the name Edgar Allan Poe in some horror movie magazines and knew he was some dead guy who had written a bunch of scary stories.

So, there I sat, cross-legged on our living room floor, with the book open across my lap. A steady stream of sunlight came through our side window from the bright summer afternoon. Dust particles danced in the light like magical sprites, setting the mood for something I hoped would be special and perhaps mystical. As things turned out, I got more than I had bargained for. I probably should have been out playing with my friends and usually would have been, but for some reason, I had found myself alone in the house, with the key to the world of terror right in my lap. My heart raced with anticipation. Perhaps that was why, while skimming through the book, I stopped at a story entitled "The Tell-Tale Heart."

I'll never know what drew me to that particular story, but within seconds, I was mesmerized, entering a world of strange, flowery language, the likes of which I had never heard. I don't know if the writing enthralled me or simply the idea that I was alone reading something I shouldn't, that I understood in advance was supposed to horrify me. All I knew was that the story did both of those things. It was like it grabbed me, held me, and although I was terrified, I couldn't stop reading it. When I reached the end, I slammed the book closed, looked around the empty living room, released an audible sigh as if I had been holding my breath for hours, and said, "Wow!"

I knew then that someday I wanted to be able to write something that would make some other inquisitive kid say, "Wow." Although I know I'll never be as eloquent as Poe, I did manage to get an interesting reaction from one of my early books. I gave a book to the woman who regularly cuts what little remains of my hair, and she gave it to her nine-year-old son, who loved horror. The best part of this story is that the boy had taken the book to school, and his teacher saw it. She paged through it and was aghast. She sent a note home with him saying that sort of book was inappropriate for his age. So not only did I manage to enthrall a young, impressionable mind, but I got to make a teacher mad at me, which I hadn't had the opportunity to do in decades. If that ain't a success, I don't know what is.

In the case of "The Tell-Tale Heart," the concept of "we never guess, we look it up" had a most unpredictable result. I could have ignored the book and accepted that he was a dead guy who wrote scary stories. Instead, I chose to find out the truth and "Look It Up." And boy, oh boy, did I learn the truth! This story fueled a lifetime of inspiration and love of the horror genre, eventually evolving me into a horror author. It's one more thing that resulted from my "growin' up Skook."

Chapter 14

There is no way anyone could grow up in Schuylkill County without having some exposure to the Polish-influenced musical style of polkas. At every wedding I attended as a kid, people danced to "The Beer Barrel Polka" or "In Heaven There Is No Beer." I always wondered why two of the most popular polkas I heard referred to beer. But, of course, not all polkas had beer references.

One of the favorite polka songs the neighborhood boys and I liked was the ever-naughty tune, "They're Always In The Way," written by Walt Solek. Although only conveyed in tongue-in-cheek double entendre, we all knew the song was talking about boobs. There's nothing that captures a young boy's attention like a boob song, even if it is a dumb polka. The chorus said, "They're always in the way," and "She's got a lot, and what she's got, they're always in the way." It was a truly entertaining tune with, for example, a verse that said, "I take my girl out walking, underneath the sky, and when I go to kiss her, they hit me in the eye," followed by the chorus.

My first exposure to playing music for people was playing in a wedding-type combination and performing an instrumental version of "In Heaven There Is No Beer." Although it was a fun piece to play, it was still a polka. It's difficult to appear cool to young girls when you're playing polkas; however, if you played in any band at any wedding, you had better know some popular polkas. Imagine being a DJ at a wedding today and not having a copy of "The Chicken Dance." Polkas were like that in the Skook; you had to play them.

Similarly, if you played at an Italian wedding in Hazelton, you had better plan on playing "The Tarantella" repeatedly until you thought your head would explode. Or if you were playing at the local fire company on Saturday night, you had to play "Wipe Out" so the local once-upon-a-time hotties, now not-so-much, could get out on the dance floor with their out-of-style bee hive hairdos and shake it for all they're worth. But back to polkas.

The radio station WMBT in Shenandoah featured a program dedicated to polkas. It was hosted by a man named Billy Urban and was called Yak Tam Billy Urban's Polka Party. Yak Tam (pronounced "Yok Tom") is Polish for "How's it going?" I have no idea how many years the program ran, but to my young ears starving for rock music, it seemed like an eternity. Billy also hosted a program called "Dial and Deal," where people could call and list a product they had for sale. Here was a typical type of call: "Hey Billy. Dzien dobry [pronounced Jane-doh-brih]. I got me a ring-ger washer fer sale right here in Shen-doe. Call 462 ..." "Dzien dobry" was Polish for "good morning." Yes, Shenandoah had a large Polish population, with more "ski's" than an Aspen, Colorado, resort.

You simply could not have lived in the Skook in the 1960s without being touched voluntarily or not by polkas.

Chapter 15

Like any small Schuylkill County town, Ashland had its share of scary, abandoned houses and ghost stories to go along with them. Many of these stories were completely fabricated from thin air and changed so many times over the years that they no longer resembled whatever the original story might have been. But that didn't stop us kids from creating our own spooky tales.

We would often sit together on someone's porch, especially on rainy days, and make up ghost stories. These tales had no basis in reality; we would simply start talking about one particular house, each of us adding his or her lies to the mix in our coal region accents.

"I heard an ax murderer kilt two kids in dat house."

"Well, my mom tolt me it was four kids dat got kilt, den da guy et dem."

"What? You mean like wanna dem dere cannibals or somptin'?"

"Yeah, I heard da bones dat da cops fount was picked clean of skin."

"They caught some bum living in the place and cookin' a leg over a fire."

"A leg? From a person? Dat can't be true."

"It's what I heard. I also heard the place is haunted wit ghosts of da kids dat got et."

"I heard dat too, an my mom said to stay away from dat place 'cause it ain't safe."

"I ain't scert 'a no ghosts. I'd walk right up and puck 'em in the pus, dat's what I'd do."

That was how our little stories would develop. And by the next time we'd get together, after each of us had plenty of time to have nightmares enough to help the tale grow. We'd either continue where we left off or start over and make up new stories. It's no wonder I wound up writing horror fiction.

We often discussed scary movies we saw at the Saturday matinees at the Roxy Theater downtown. Even though everybody saw the same film, often together, we always seemed to start the conversation by asking, "Did you see the part where ..." When you think about that statement, you realize how ridiculous it was. Of course they "saw the part where ..." They were in the same theater as you, sitting right next to you, watching the same movie. They had to "see the part where ..." Yet time and time again, when we discussed a movie's finer points, we always started by saying, "Did you see the part where ..."

Probably, the only thing we enjoyed more than initially watching the movie was talking about it ad nauseam afterward. That was when we could discuss details like, "Did you see the part where that guy's guts flopped out of his stomach?" Or perhaps we would ask, "Did you see the part where the guy's head got cut off? I wonder how they did that." Oh, the joys of being a junior student of the fine art of cinema analysis.

Sometimes, we would be so bold as to offer unsolicited criticism and say, "If I was makin' dat movie, I would have ended it different. That ending stunk!" Someone else would chime in and say, "Yeah, me too. Day shoulda kilt dat ugly guy at da end." Little did I know at that age that I would be carrying on such criticism my entire life until, one day, I had enough and decided to write my own stories. Now, people can read my stories and say, "That ending stunk!" For the record, sometimes they do. Such is the legacy of my Skook horror experiences.

Chapter 16

The night before Halloween in our little town was known to us kids as Mischief Night. It was also misunderstood by us. You see, since it had that name and everyone we knew was aware of it, we assumed, as the stupid kids we were, that it meant it was ok for us to go about town creating mischief. Not that we went around starting fires or burning buildings like they did in Detroit on their annual Devil's Night. Our Mischief Night was much less interesting than that. We didn't even toilet paper houses and trees or do the flaming bag of poo on the porch thing that you see in movies. We were a lot more boring than that.

Some bigger and faster kids might ring someone's doorbell and then run away. The important thing here was not only speed but timing. Yes, you had to be fast enough to get out of sight before the neighbor answered his door, but it was also critical *when* you rang the doorbell. For instance, if three or four kids had hit the house before you and you were unaware of this important fact, it would most definitely spell trouble for you. The homeowner might be standing right behind the door waiting for you, the next culprit.

Since our town was small and this was the 1960s, just about everyone knew everyone else, including their kids. So, if you were unfortunate enough to be the fifth kid to ring the doorbell, chances were the homeowner would be waiting, opening the door, identifying you, and contacting your parents via the secret parental network. I'm told this doorbell ringing practice now has the name "ding dong ditch." We were never clever enough to have come up with such a name. For us, it was just called, "ring the doorbell and run."

We had another opportunity for mischief for smaller kids who might not yet be ready to ring doorbells. We could go around soaping up car windows. We believed we could do this without getting in trouble because it was Mischief Night. That made it legal in our goofy little minds. It also didn't take into account that if someone caught you soaping their windows, they might opt to beat your sorry butt for the fun of it. So, whether it was Mischief Night or not, we knew we had to be careful.

One Halloween Eve, probably when I was about nine or ten, I was planning what mischief to perform. I remember my grandmother, Lucy Metzinger, dropped off a special bag of stuff for us to use on Mischief Night. She had saved all the small remnants of the soap bars she had used over the year and put them all in a plastic bag. Since she worked at the Marko Town House, she also managed to put in some of those tiny hotel bars of soap. I had no idea my gram could be so cool. This was awesome, and it seemed to validate the legality of Mischief Night.

I decided to do something special and maybe even naughty for Mischief Night that year. I was never one of those kids who had the patience to work for a long time soaping a window. Some kids did and would put such a thick layer of soap on the car windows that it practically had to be scraped off. Not me. In my opinion, that was boring and took way too much time. If you took too long to do something like that, there was a chance you could get caught. And getting caught meant taking a whooping from someone, which was not for skinny little me. I wanted to move in, do the soaping, and move on.

So, I devised what I considered an ingenious plan. Like the modern-day taggers who spray paint their logos on city buildings, I came up with a design that I could use that would be quick, effective, and maybe even a little dirty. I decided that my insignia for that Mischief Night would be a butt. That's right. I came up with a gluteus maximus design that I thought would be offensive, and it was one I could do quickly and safely. It was a circle with a curve down the middle representing the crack. I could draw one of those on a window in about two seconds and then move on to the next vehicle.

I thought I had devised a clever design to soap onto the car windows.

Sadly, this exercise meant to upset the entire town was an abysmal failure. It never occurred to me that after drawing several dozen or maybe one hundred of these stylized backsides on car windows all over town, no one but me would have any idea what that symbol represented. Someone might be a bit upset that someone scribbled on their window and they had to clean it off, but the entire butt crack reference was lost. I suppose, in hindsight (pun intended), it might be enough that I knew what it meant.

This did not deter me from participating in future Mischief Night events for the years to come; however, the failure of the posterior presentation made me go back to simply scribbling on windows for the remainder of my mischievous years.

We used to do something mischievous for fun, not just on Mischief Night, but any night we were bored and wanted to do something mischievous. We would try to get someone to chase us. On the surface, that seems harmless enough, but if you consider what we did to get someone to chase us, you might think we were out of our little minds.

The simplest way we initiated a chase was to wait until some young hoodlum with his souped-up chick magnet came driving up one of our neighborhood streets. Then, when he passed by, we would shout, "Junk it! Buy a horse!" Depending upon who the potential psycho was who happened to be driving that night, the car would stop and start backing up. That was our cue to scramble, and like cockroaches suddenly frightened by bright light, we would head in all directions.

The car would drive around the neighborhood looking for us. If the car had many passengers, they would pile out and run after us. This was a major adrenalin rush because it would not be pretty if they caught any of us. There were tales of kids being smacked around after being caught. But the worst thing I ever heard was kids being "pantsed." That meant that when they were caught, they were dragged into the car and then taken up into the abandoned strip mines where their pants and underpants were removed, and they were forced to walk home in that humiliating condition.

I never knew of anyone who had been caught and treated to such indignities, but just the idea that it might happen was enough to send the danger and excitement level through the roof. One of the guys had the bright idea for us to get chased by the local police since they would neither beat us nor pants us. So, a bunch of us would stand in the shadows until we saw a police cruiser coming in the distance, and when his lights were almost on us, we would all run away as if we had just been up to something illegal. On occasion, the police car would drive around the neighborhood looking for us, even sometimes shining search lights into places we might have hidden. Talk about a major rush!

Another thing I never did but was told some of the other guys did was what we called "Chippy Chasin'." The way that worked was you went to a location known for being a place where teenage boys

94

and girls went in their cars to "make out." When you found a vehicle with the windows steamed up, you banged on the window and ran away. This was probably one of the most dangerous forms of mischief as we were all certain that getting caught Chippy Chasin' would result in you getting a severe beating. I never knew of anyone who had been caught, but the idea of that level of danger created many exciting opportunities for mischief.

Speaking of which, here's an interesting thing we did one Mischief Night. Someone had made a dummy from old clothes stuffed with rags. A group of us positioned ourselves on top of a wall that ran along the part of Eighth Street close to the high school. We planned to wait until we saw a car coming up the street and then throw the dummy down onto the roadway. The idea was the driver might think a kid jumped onto the street and hit the kid with his car. As if that plan was not twisted enough, one of our tribe of miscreants decided to pee all over the pants of the dummy before dropping it.

As things worked out, a car approached, the dummy went down, the car stopped, the driver got out, and the driver bent over to check on the "victim's" welfare. When he first realized that the victim was a dummy, we heard an assortment of interesting curses. Then, when the driver realized why his hands were wet after checking on the alleged victim, he really let loose with a string of profanities, most of which were missed as we were already high-tailing it out of the area. Such were the kinds of things that happened when groups of boys became bored on Mischief Night in the Skook.

Chapter 17

I have many fond memories of Christmas time in the Skook. As little kids, Christmas was a magical time for all of us neighborhood kids. It was a time when we believed Santa Claus really brought gifts for us all on Christmas Eve. Our poor parents never got credit for any of the amazing things they did.

For example, my folks would put up our real Christmas tree on Christmas Eve but didn't decorate it. They always placed it in the dining room between our closet door on the left and the entrance to the kitchen on the right. Then, after all of us kids went to bed, they would add the lights, ornaments, and tinsel so that when we came down on Christmas morning, the first thing we would see when we came down the stairs to the living room was the magnificent site of the fully decorated, sparkling Christmas tree. I have to admit, it was breathtaking to behold. Then, we would see the wrapped presents under the tree and adjust our priorities accordingly.

Still, in hindsight, what I remember most about those early Christmas mornings weren't the presents or the partially eaten cookies and milk I left for Santa but the incredible and magical sight of that illuminated tree. I recall asking my mom how Santa had time to decorate our tree with all the work he had to do delivering presents. She told me he simply stood in front of the tree, raised his arms, and a second later, the tree was finished. Having decorated more than my share of trees over the years, I appreciate how they took the time to make Christmas even more magical for us. This exemplifies how amazing things can be accomplished with little money but lots of love.

I remember the day one of my friends told me there was no such thing as Santa Claus. I told him he was a liar, and then, being quite upset, I went home and told my mom what he said. My mom explained that Santa Claus was a spirit, just like God was a spirit, so if my friend didn't believe in Santa, then he didn't believe in God.

Armed with this new knowledge, I confronted my friend and confidently said, "Santa Claus is a spirit, and God is a spirit, so if you don't believe in Santa, then you don't believe in God." I felt like I had delivered the winning blow until he said with his own brand of confidence, "I'm fine with that since I don't believe in God, either." I walked away completely disarmed and unaware of how to deal with that last statement.

My Aunt Jean and Uncle Alex Bovidge had one of those really cool aluminum Christmas trees. I always thought those were the neatest things I had ever seen, especially when she turned on the red, green, yellow, and blue rotating spotlight that made the silver tree reflect and change colors. Years later, when I started playing in local rock bands, I wished I had one or two of those babies to shine on the band during our performances. Instead, I ended up making wooden boxes, painting them black, and, with my pitifully limited electrical experience, wiring them for colored spotlights.

When my folks eventually got our first artificial Christmas tree, I was a young teenager. The duty of putting the thing together fell to me. It was the type of tree with a two-inch diameter painted green dowel about six feet long that contained a series of holes drilled at angles into the dowel. These holes were to receive individual branches that came with the tree. Each branch had a bent wire at the end to fit into the appropriate hole, and each wire was painted with a color code.

The instructions provided showed the assembler which color went with which row of holes. The objective was that upon insertion of the appropriate colored bent branch wire into the proper angle hole, the result would eventually become a Christmas tree. I followed the instructions and painstakingly installed branch after branch, row after row until the tree was complete. I probably should have stepped back and examined the tree periodically during the assembly process; however, I neglected that step. The result was that when I was finished and finally did step back to give my project a once-over, I discovered I had somehow assembled the tree upside down.

Instead of looking like a magical wonder of yuletide cheer, my tree looked like an upside down, bushy triangle. After several minutes of head scratching, I realized I had no choice but to pull out all the branches, set them aside by color marking, and then start over, doing the reverse of what I had just done. That worked fine, duh!

Instead of looking like a magical wonder of yuletide cheer, my tree looked like an upside down, bushy triangle.

Chapter 18

Every hormonal boy with a pulse in eighth grade, including me, was in love, or at least in lust, with our new art teacher, who I'll simply refer to as Miss Barbie, even though that wasn't her name. She was, however, fresh out of college, blonde, and cute as cute could be. As if that wasn't enough, she had a wonderful personality and was the favorite of both the boys and girls in class. I can't recall all the details of those art classes as I was probably spending all my time mooning like the love-struck schoolboy I was and drooling into my watercolors.

One of the few things I do recall was winning an award for my Halloween window painting that year, a psychedelic jack-o'-lantern that I painted on Danny's Drive-In Restaurant window at the south end of town. Eventually, eighth grade was over, and life moved on; I advanced from grade to grade and never saw Miss Barbie again.

That was until that sad and heartbreaking day several years later when that same lovely teacher unknowingly shattered my fragile young heart into smithereens. I was probably a junior in high school then and played guitar with a wedding band from Mahanoy City. As I recall, we were providing music for a wedding in the Hometown area. Things were going according to schedule, and it was time to bring in the bride and groom. Our band struck up some introductory tune as the happy couple made their way into the venue and walked toward the head table.

I stood staring in shocked horror. Yep, you guessed it. It was our precious Miss Barbie, now Mrs. somebody or other, with her new, completely unworthy husband, Ken. Somehow, I kept playing, even with my stomach in knots and my heart broken in two. I swear, somewhere in the cosmos of time and space, I heard the cry of a hundred eighth grade boys as their hearts were systematically torn from their chests. Okay, so maybe I'm overdramatizing a bit. But it was nonetheless traumatic for my young and fragile psyche.

To make matters worse, ninth grade art class was nothing like the almost heavenly experience of the previous year. We were cursed with a strange art teacher, who may have only lasted a year or so to the best of my memory. Maybe she was a substitute; I can't recall, but I certainly hope she was. She was the complete opposite of our wonderful Miss Barbie. Not just because she was old and miserable but also because she reminded me of the Wicked Witch of the West, and I told you how I felt about that character. I couldn't wrap my head around the idea that she might have been teaching art anywhere as a career. For this story, I'll simply call her Miss Witch even though I have no idea if she was a Miss or a Mrs. However, I have to think that the concept of some poor working slob coming home after a hard day on the job to that woman must have been a fate worse than death for him.

I can't recall many details of that year in art class as, for the most part, it was uneventful, which is what leads me to assume she must have been a substitute, just putting in time and collecting a check until it was time to hop on her broom and fly off to the next group of unsuspecting students. That said, one incident sticks in my mind as it was the only time I recall ever interacting directly with her.

Remember that I was still enjoying the effects of having my Halloween window painting winning an award the previous year and had been actively practicing my drawing and cartooning. I thought I was well on the way to being a fairly good artist. That was until my encounter with Miss Witch. If I remember correctly, our assignment was to paint some fish swimming in the water. It must have been during my darker periods of painting. Don't judge me; if Picasso could have his blue period, then I was entitled to have my dark period.

All I remember is that I painted the water in shades of dark purple, and my fish were opaque gray and black. I considered it a good example of a mood piece, symbolizing all my early teen angst. Honestly, I had no idea what symbolism was, let alone what angst might have been; I simply wasn't that sophisticated. For whatever

102

reason, I wanted to paint that particular work the way I did. I didn't give it much thought or consideration; I simply painted what I felt. I believed that was what art was supposed to be about. I honestly thought that despite her miserable face and hostile demeanor, Miss Witch would take one look at my masterpiece, fall to her knees in adoration, and immediately recommend the painting be sent to the Philadelphia Museum of Art,where it would be displayed for all the world to enjoy.

To my shock and dismay, she took one look at the painting, turned to me, and asked, "What is this? Are you retarded?"

That's right. A junior high school teacher actually asked her student if he was retarded. Not only would that be considered incredibly inappropriate in today's more politically correct society, but even back in 1969 or 1970, it was far from something any educator should have said. For a moment, I was taken aback and unable to comprehend what she had just said. Did she really just ask me if I was retarded? I may not be the sharpest bulb in the shed, and I may not have been Alfred Einstein, but I was fairly certain I was not mentally deficient. Then again, if I was, would I know it? I was momentarily bathed in a wash of uncertainty and confusion, but then I came to my senses.

What I did next probably could have gotten me expelled or at least sent to the principal's office, but neither occurred. My immediate response was more out of anger and hurt than anything. I looked at her and said, "No, I'm not. But I think you are." I realize this was not a creatively profound comeback, akin to, "I know you are, but what am I?" But, hey. I was only a punk kid with a limited Skook education at that time, being called retarded by a teacher.

Holy crap! As soon as I said that, I figured I was a dead kid walking, but nothing happened. She simply turned and walked away. Nothing else happened then or later, to the best of my recollection. I didn't get expelled, put in detention, or get a failing grade. Maybe a mark was placed on my dreaded "permanent record," you know, the one that teachers threaten will follow you all your life. Perhaps she realized her mistake and decided it would be better to let it go and hope that I wasn't one of those kids who complained to his parents and had them contact the school board. I wasn't, and they didn't.

Still, to this day, I have a hard time believing this was the sort of thing I encountered during my formative years in school. Somehow, I survived with only minimal damage to my ego. The truth was, at that age, it would have taken a lot more than that to damage my overconfident ego. Lack of self-esteem was never an issue for me.

Chapter 19

Corporal punishment was a way of life in many Skook school districts in the 1960s. Every teacher had his or her own custom-modified paddle for students who got out of line. I should point out that "getting out of line" was mostly subjective. It was up to the paddle-wielding teacher to determine where that "line" was and how far it had been crossed. Also, the location of that line varied not only from teacher to teacher but from day to day and sometimes from hour to hour. All it took was a teacher arguing with his or her spouse at breakfast that morning or with someone at school to put a student on the wrong side of that line without even knowing why.

In addition, some teachers were sick and sadistic freaks who took what I considered way too much pleasure in bringing pain to students. Remember, many of these teachers were once the nerdy "smart kids" who happened to attend the same Skook school where they now taught. This was the same school where they were regularly subjected to unimaginable daily pain and torture at the hands of sadomasochistic knuckle-dragging, mouth-breathing bullies. Now, not only were they in charge, but they had the power and were armed with death sticks. They were given the authority to use these weapons of pain whenever and however they saw fit.

Take, for example, this completely fictitious scenario. Suppose it's the first day of junior high, and you see your new math teacher standing at the front of the room, leaning against his desk with his arms crossed. A wooden paddle is lying across his desk, painted gloss black with red paint splotches, simulating blood splatter strategically placed at potential paddle points of impact. On the blackboard, the teacher's name is written in white chalk. For this example, let's call him the fictitious Mr. Denkel. That name Denkel sounds familiar, but you can't pinpoint where you might have heard it.

Mr. Denkel reads his class roster and notices a surname he recognizes, which, unfortunately for you, happens to be your name. Let's assume that your name is John Doe. He calls your name, and when you raise your hand, he says, "Good morning, John, and how are you today?"

Although his voice seems cordial on the surface, you sense something foul and evil lurking below. You suspect this might be, and likely is, some sort of trap. You cautiously offer, "I'm fine."

"What an interesting name you have there, John. By some chance, is your father's name Charles Doe."

"Um ... Not my father, but I did have an uncle, Chuck." You reply, feeling the trap closing in on you, getting ready to spring any second.

"Did have?" The teacher asks, his eyes growing wider by the second.

You reply cautiously, "Um, yes. Uncle Chuck was killed a few years ago in a motorcycle accident."

"Oh, I'm so sorry to hear that, John." Mr. Denkel says, not looking in the least bit sorry. If anything, the man seems frighteningly happy. He continues to smile at you with a grin that looks not only forced but borderline insane. The Joker in your *Batman* comics looks more normal than what you are witnessing on the face of this closet loonie.

Then Mr. Denkel springs the trap and says, "I believe I might have known your uncle in junior high school."

Then it all comes flooding back, and you recall your late Uncle Chuck telling you about the skinny little nerd he used to torture in junior high. "His name was Denkel, but we called him Denkelberries. You know, like dingleberries," Chuck had said proudly. Then he told about the time he gave Denkelberries a wedgie so intense that the elastic band of the kid's tighty-whities reached all the way up to his neck. "He must have been wearing his old man's bloomers for them to stretch up that high," Chuck insisted as he laughed hysterically.

106

If there is some twisted moral to this tale, it would be when a nerdy kid becomes a paddle-wielding teacher with authority, the sins of the predecessors will be paid for with the stinging flesh of those descendants who follow. Although this particular account was a work of fiction, you can see how, in reality, corporal punishment can easily go very wrong.

Regarding those butt-smacking weapons of darkness, I believe the paddles used in our schools were manufactured in the wood shop in the school's basement. Our shop teacher had many side projects, and paddle-making was likely one of them. Paddle modification was probably another, such as drilling holes to make paddles more aerodynamic and increase pain. Some teachers had students sign their paddles after getting a taste of the sting; others decorated their paddles with words or images to strike fear into the hearts of potentially bad students.

I recall the numerous stories of the legendary paddle owned and operated by our junior high school principal. His nickname was "Bullet" because of the deadly speed at which he could swing his paddle, which it was said had had many of those holes mentioned earlier drilled into the paddle to reduce wind resistance and increase sting-ability. Legend boasted that anyone bad enough to be sent to the principal's office and receive a taste of his paddle of death would never be the same. Like the great god Thor with his mighty hammer, it was said that Bullet could bring even the biggest, toughest, and most criminally insane students to tears with just one swing of his deadly butt slammer.

If you've ever seen the television program Scared Straight, where they bring out insane-looking convicts to terrify and convince marginal young people to avoid a life of crime by telling them horrifying stories of prison life, you would know how effective the legendary stories of what went on inside the principal's office were at keeping the uncaged animals in my junior high in check. If anyone saw some borderline psychopath being led to Bullet's office, it wouldn't surprise anyone if someone shouted, "Dead man walking."

There was another aspect of corporal punishment that needs to be mentioned, and that's where what I call the "Pervert Factor" rears its ugly head. There were no guidelines on how hard or soft to swing a paddle, so often, certain teachers would give girls, especially pretty and prematurely developed girls, a light tap with their paddles. So, you might ask, what's wrong with that? Well, that's where the "pervert factor" comes into play.

Here we have a degenerate middle-aged former jock who has never mentally given up his "big man on campus" attitude and still thinks that junior high school girls find him all that and a bag of chips. He notices a really attractive girl with a short skirt and big mockatushkies talking in class and decides it's time for him to have some fun. He calls her to come up to the front of the room to get paddled.

She giggles because she's played this game before. The teacher sternly tells her to face the class and bend over to receive her punishment. Then, after a few seconds of his heavy breathing, he gives her a gentle tap with his paddle on the white, ruffled panties he's been ogling, which she put on just for this occasion. She walks back to her desk, feigning hurt, but knowing this little "extra credit" will guarantee her an "A" on her report card. This, my friends, is the "pervert factor."

Those of us who were of the X-Y chromosomes had seen this occur countless times with many teachers, not just young teachers but lecherous older perverts as well. Unfortunately, unlike the previously stated young ladies with their double X chromosome, we never got a break and often got to feel the full impact of any paddling we were subjected to. No mercy was ever offered, regardless of the unseen underwear we happened to be wearing.

My older sister, Georgine, told me a story once that I hope wasn't exaggerated too much, but sometimes kids tend to make stories a bit more dramatic in the retelling. I'm as guilty of that as anyone. As the story was relayed to me, one horny teacher, fitting the above middle-aged flabby-butt loser description, made the mistake of trying this panty-paddle routine on Jeanie once. Anyone who knew my sister knew that messing with her was like messing with a wild panther. Things never ended well. The teacher, unfortunately, was unaware he was about to pull the pin on a live hand grenade. The result he received was not something he had ever expected.

I'm not sure what Jeanie's alleged infraction might have been, but it likely involved talking during class. She was and still is a great talker. The teacher, a washed-up has-been former jock turned less-than-mediocre educator, ordered Jeanie to come up to the front of the class. This jerk told her to face the class, bend over, and accept her punishment. He had been using this routine for years, and no one ever complained. Kids were afraid to go up against a teacher, especially a popular one. Jeanie wore a skirt that day and had heard of the teacher's reputation. There was no way she would let this freak have his way.

"Face the class and bend over," the degenerate said as he tapped his paddle menacingly into the palm of his left hand.

Jeanie angrily replied, "No!"

"What did you say?," he asked with disbelief.

Jeanie replied, "I said, 'No, I won't bend over.'"

"I'm your teacher, and I told you to bend over."

"No. And you can't make me," she insisted.

Then he got an idea to threaten her to get her to comply, "If you disobey me, I'll have no choice but to send you to the principal's office. You don't want that, do you?"

Jeanie left the classroom and, as she closed the door, said, "Yes, I do. And I'm gonna tell him that you're a weirdo pervert who likes looking at girls' panties. You better hope I don't get sent home because if I tell my dad, he'll come in here and bash your face in."

I never learned how that turned out, but I suspect the teacher might have had his paddle taken away after a serious "Come to Jesus" meeting with the principal. Who knows? Things like that never seemed to get properly punished back in those days.

The years went by, the times changed, and corporal punishment became a thing of the past, as extinct as the Dodo bird. Maybe that was a good thing.

Chapter 20

I'd like to take a little time to discuss a humiliating but apparently necessary ritual we poor and unsuspecting boys had to go through in 1967 or so when we were attempting to try out for our local midget football teams. First, I should apologize to all the "little people" everywhere. In the twenty-first century, the term "midget" can be construed as callous, insensitive, or offensive, and it is far from politically correct, but I assure you I mean no disrespect. Back in 1967, when our local young peoples' football league was formed, that's what it was called — midget football. So, since the gist of this story has very little (no pun intended) to do with the term midget itself, I beg your indulgence and hope you can forgive this slight, small as it may be (pun intended).

When news that our town was forming a midget football league hit the streets, it bounced from kid to kid, as such news always does in small towns. It didn't matter that there were no cellphones, no personal computers, and no internet; word spread by kid-net. And there was no need to pick up the phone and call each other, either. We all played outside in the streets and had friends all over town. It was more akin to that scene from Disney's 101 Dalmatians animated movie where news goes from one barking dog to the next, and soon every dog in town is howling the news.

Of course, when my friends and I heard about the league, we were pretty excited. We had been playing touch football in the streets of our neighborhoods for years. In fact, each neighborhood had its own informal teams, and we often got together with opposing teams and had our own pickup games. There were the Arch Street Angels, the Brock Street Bulldogs, and the Market Street Mauraders, to name a few. But these were strictly pickup teams and completely disorganized.

At this point, I should mention to those who didn't know me back then that I was one of our neighborhood team's most pathetic football players. This went hand-in-hand with my lack of ability to play baseball, basketball, or any other sport I attempted to participate in. Some people whine about being the last person picked for a team. In my case, I was never actually picked, even if I was the last.

It was more like, "We don't want him, you take him," and, "We don't want him either, you take him." Or, "Come on, give us a break. We had him last time."

I always thought it was great having teams fighting over me, even if they were fighting not to take me. How pathetic is that? Maybe it wasn't that bad, but sometimes it felt that way.

However, I refused to admit defeat. I figured if I just kept trying and working harder and harder, then eventually, I would overcome my clumsiness and find some sport that I didn't completely stink at. What did the cartoon character Underdog, voiced by actor Wally Cox, always say? "If at first you fail your deed, try again till you succeed."

I just knew that if I put my mind to it, put my heart and soul into it, and tried with everything I had, I might rise to a level of humiliating mediocracy. But I quickly learned that even setting the bar that low, success was only the sort of thing that happens on the Hallmark Channel or after school specials. Reality ain't so pretty.

It took me several more years to finally throw in the towel and admit I had no business participating in any sport. I probably should have realized whenever the only person cut from school sports tryouts was me that maybe the universe, in all its cruel and painful wisdom, was trying to tell me something.

So, as a young lad, still living the fantasy that I actually had a place in the world of physical confrontation, I embraced the opportunity to once again fail miserably at yet another sport. I registered for the Midget Football League and learned I had to take a physical exam before starting. I filled out the application myself and then asked my parents to sign it, giving me permission to try out. My mom was against it, assuming, based on past experience, that I'd likely end up broken into a dozen or more assorted pieces. Dad assured her no such thing would happen to me as I would probably never make the team in the first place.

I realize his statement may not sound very supportive or might be construed as insensitive, but this was a different time when parents told it like it was. This was back when youth sports had winners and losers, when the best players played and the worst players warmed the bench. This was back when we actually kept score, and only the truly deserving got trophies. Yeah, I know it sounds like an exaggerated tale told by an old fart, but so be it.

As I said, my dad was just being honest with me. On the positive side, he gave me a good pep talk I never forgot. He said, "Look, Son, being good at sports is no big deal. Even the best players out there are washed up by thirty. Then all they can do is sit around watching sports on TV and getting fat. But you can play guitar. And you'll be able to do that all your life, even when you're an old man." Dad was certainly right about that.

But I digress. The point is, I had no idea exactly what the term "physical exam" meant or what I would be required to do, but I figured, "How bad could it be?" I'd been to the doctor before, where he listened to my heart and checked my ears and throat; no biggie, right? But I soon learned this was not simply going to the doctor and getting a paper signed; this was an army-style "turn your head and cough" mass physical for all registered players.

As fate would have it, on the day of the physical, I found myself standing in the high school gym in a line of about fifty or more boys between the ages of twelve and thirteen. I held tightly to my signed permission slip as I waited for my turn to see the doctor at the front of the line, who was sitting on a low stool ... for whatever reason. I had no idea how he would check my ears and throat from down there, but he was the doctor; he'd have to figure that out.

Speaking of the doctor, the one they had chosen that day was a grumpy local doctor whom some of my friends went to regularly. They all were terrified of him because he had the reputation of "giving needles" for every ailment, no matter how minor. Got a headache? He had a shot for that. Vomiting, diarrhea? He had a shot for that. Stuffy head, sore throat? Drop your drawers, bend over, and take a needle for that too. I wasn't a fan of injections, especially those rendered upon my "gluteus maximum," as I liked to call my butt. Fortunately, my folks took me to another doctor, and thanks to my being allergic to penicillin, the cure-all drug of the day, I rarely got shots.

Being the curious kid I was, I glanced up toward the front of the line to see what was happening. I stared in shocked disbelief at what I saw. The kid at the front of the line was standing with his pants and underwear pulled down to the floor, and the doctor was touching him. What the heck was going on? I couldn't ever recall any doctor feeling me down there before. I didn't know what I was supposed to do. Should I leave, go home, and tell my mom?

She had always warned me not to talk to strangers or get in their cars, and never let them see or touch my "birdie." Yet here we were, fifty or more young boys lined up, waiting for some grumpy old coot to manhandle our stuff. Thank goodness there were no girls around. I glanced about the gym to make sure. This wasn't entirely true since the doctor's nurse was standing next to him, and even though she was old, like grandma old, she was technically not a guy.

That was when I heard a rumble of whispers working their way back through the line. The kid in the line in front of me turned and said, "He's checking us for hernia. Pass it on." Being true to the kid network, I turned and conveyed the message to the kid behind me. I did so with calm conviction as if I were as knowledgeable as any sophisticated young man. All the while inside, my brain was screaming, "What the heck is a hernia? And what does it have to do with some doctor grabbing my balls?"

114

I was just about ready to step out of line and run home when I glanced toward the front and saw a kid who I'll give a fictitious name for this story. This is for two very important reasons. First, I wouldn't want to cause the kid any unnecessary embarrassment, and second, I honestly can't recall who the kid was. Several personalities in that gymnasium fit that description, and rather than guess incorrectly, I'll just make up the name Marshall. For the record, I don't know, nor have I ever known, anyone named Marshall.

Marshall was one of the bigger boys in our class, and as the line progressed, he was working his way to the front. It was obvious that Marshall was much more physically developed than my other friends and me. I don't know if he was older than us, but it was not uncommon for some parents to start their kids in school a bit later. It was also possible Marshall had been "held back" a grade. Whatever the situation, he was taller, more muscular, and already had a deeper voice than the rest of us.

Before long, it was his turn at the front. Marshall approached the doctor, appearing to have all the confidence in the world. I wished then I could be more like Marshall. As Marshall dropped his jeans, an audible gasp could be heard echoing from the front of the line and reverberating throughout the gymnasium. The old nurse was staring down at Marshall, her mouth agape and her eyes bugging out from behind her catseye glasses. She also had a bit of a pleased expression for some reason I didn't understand then. Within seconds, the kid network was thrust into high gear, and the ever-important message made its way back to my spot in the line.

"Marshall's got hair down there! A whole bunch of it! And he's got a really big thing, too! It looks like an anteater's nose, or maybe an elephant's trunk... pass it on!"

Not sure what to make of this news, I dutifully turned to pass the message to the boy behind me, but he must have heard the kid in front of me because he was already turned around, sharing the news. I considered that a blessing because it wasn't what I felt comfortable saying. How could Marshall be "big" and have "hair" down south? God knows I didn't fit that description, and I was fairly sure most of my other friends didn't, either. We were all just boys. That sort of thing was man stuff, or at least high school boy stuff. We were just getting ready to start seventh grade.

I imagine right about now, any man reading this account all these years later is puffing out his chest and thinking, "Yep. I have no doubt he's talking about me. I'm the mysterious Marshall he's telling this story about." Dream on, Pee Wee. Neither you nor I nor 98 percent of us in that line fit that description.

Now, back to the story. I looked down toward the front of the line and saw Marshall walking away with confidence, obviously pleased with the impression he had made. The next kid in line was reluctantly dropping his drawers. Following an act like Marshall and his anaconda was a nightmare come true for that poor kid. I saw the old nurse trying desperately to suppress a grin. That kid wore a crew cut then, and even from my spot in line, I could see his head blushing crimson.

"That poor guy," I thought. Then, as the line continued to inch forward, I thought, "Poor me! I wasn't any better off than any of the other boys in the genital endowment arena. Being painfully modest, even though our bathroom door was perpendicular to the door in my bedroom at home, I wouldn't try to dash to the bathroom without being adequately covered. I had always managed to hide things of that nature from my friends. But in this environment, all bets would be off. The line had gotten progressively shorter, and although plenty of boys were behind me, I was glad all those before me would be gone when I had to drop my drawers. I considered doing the only thing I could think of and asking the person behind me to take my spot. Then, maybe I could do it repeatedly until I eventually found myself at the back of the line. But I realized no one in line was any more eager to get to the front than I was.

As is always true, all good things had to end, and eventually, I found myself standing terrified and staring into the doctor's grumpy face. He was a grizzled old cuss who looked like he hated this as much as we did. I was concerned that, in his frustration, the old doctor might grab my little boys too hard and pop them like two grapes. Since I hadn't heard anyone else screaming in agony, however, I assumed I was in good hands, so to speak. Reluctantly, I handed him my permission slip and then stood in paralytic terror.

"Drop 'em," the doctor demanded in a simultaneously stern and uninterested voice, "Jeans and underpants. To the floor."

"Drop 'em. Jeans and underpants. To the floor."

I hesitated for a second or two, which seemed like an eternity. Finally, Nurse Grandma said, "Come on, kid. It's already been a long day. Time's a'wastin'."

Finally, I unbuckled my belt, unhooked my jeans, and, closing my eyes, dropped them both to the ground. I felt two icy hands grabbing my minuscule equipment as the doctor said, "Turn your head and cough."

I had no idea why he wanted me to cough. I mean, what was the point of that? And why did I have to turn my head? Was there some muscle that went from my marbles to my neck and activated when I turned my head? And did that magic muscle tell the doctor if I had a hernia, whatever the heck a hernia was?

I didn't dare ask, so I turned my head to the left and coughed as instructed. He still had those icy fingers around my jewels, and as soon as he let go, I felt like the weight of the world had been lifted from my young shoulders.

"Pull up your drawers; you're done," the doctor said.

I pulled up my pants, zipped up, and headed for the door. Thank goodness the gym was mostly empty. No matter my fate regarding midget football, I knew fifty of my comrades and I would never think of Marshall quite the same after that day.

And, as you may have already presumed, I was predictably cut from the team after several days of tryouts. At least this time, I wasn't alone; a dozen or so kids were cut along with me. So, only slightly dejected, I went home and played my guitar.

Chapter 21

This is a story about a booger stuck to a wall. If this sounds like it might be a somewhat disgusting story, it kind of is. But it is also a bit funny and ironic. So, if you have a delicate stomach and fear you might be bothered by such a topic, feel free to skip over this; however, for those of us with an arrested development that stopped somewhere around the age of thirteen, it might prove bizarrely interesting. This is also true for those readers who, despite their repulsion, are morbidly curious.

The story starts like this. It was spring at school, and there were only a few weeks until summer break. A bunch of us were waiting outside our homeroom door for the day's last class to end. As we stood patiently waiting, one of the boys noticed something.

"Hey, look. Someone wiped a boogie on the wall," he said.

We looked, and he was right. Someone had wiped a good-sized nose goblin on the wall a few inches from the left side door trim and about head height. It was quite a prize specimen, hitting us simultaneously with the mixed feelings of fascination and revulsion.

"Ugh, that's disgusting," one of the girls in line said.

Another boy said, "Yeah, it is, but it's kinda funny, too."

"It's not funny, it's gross."

Another boy suggested, "Perhaps gross, but it makes a statement, too."

"A statement?" Another girl suggested, clearly looking like she might lose her lunch.

"Well, I suppose it's like a protest. You know, an 'up yours' to the school and the authorities."

A boy who came up to investigate took a closer look, studying it much too thoroughly, in my opinion, and said, "Nope. I don't think so. It just looks like a boogie to me." He seemed to analyze it like a research scientist, spending far too much time looking it over. Then he shocked everyone by taking a pen, drawing a circle around the mucus glob, and then writing the word "boogie" on the wall with an arrow pointing to the circle. "There, that should be sufficient." He said.

"What the heck did you do that for?," someone asked.

He replied, "Isn't it obvious? Now the janitor or a teacher will see the gross thing and maybe clean it off." I thought about it and then realized he might be right. It sounded like a good and logical idea to me at the time. But we were to discover that logic had no standing when it came to goober artwork.

The door to the homeroom opened, the students streamed out, and we entered to wrap up our day and head home. I had forgotten about the nose-picked Picasso until the next day. When I approached homeroom the next morning, I saw some additional graffiti had been placed around the object. One said, "snot," another said, "gross," and perhaps the most revolting said, "Jim's lunch." I don't know which Jim in the school the message referred to, but this culinary declaration was far from complimentary.

I was certain that with the additional writing on the wall, someone would contact the janitorial staff to come out, remove the offensive object, and clean off or perhaps paint over the even more offensive graffiti. But by the end of the day, as I approached homeroom, not only was it still there, but even more writing had been added. Gems like, "It's a 'booger,' not a 'boogie,'" or the pun, "I thought it was blood, but it's not." I thought the last play on words was particularly entertaining, as "it's not" meant "it's snot."

Within a few weeks, the graffiti had grown to cover an oval area about a foot wide and two feet tall. It looked like a spider web of obnoxious sayings and funny cartoons all focused around the circular area in the center of the mass. For the record, none of the graffiti or cartoons were mine. It's not that I was a goody-two-shoes or anything like that. I just liked living and feared my folks would kill me if they found out I did something like that.

120

I couldn't for the life of me understand how that disgusting piece of nose jelly, not to mention a giant mass of writing that rivaled the worst graffiti in the most rundown bathroom in the school, still was displayed almost proudly on the wall. I was sure the homeroom teacher had to have seen it, along with most of the kids in the school. Word about something as gross as that would have spread through the school like wildfire, and it did. The place sort of became a shrine or tribute to student nasal rebellion. Almost every kid in the school knew about it and would make a pilgrimage to see the miraculous display like cave explorers discovering the paintings of ancient man.

Soon, the school year was over, and we said goodbye to each other and the booger wall to be off for our summer vacation. Of course, we were all so busy over the summer enjoying ourselves as we always did that those thoughts of the wall and the booger faded from our minds. Summer vacation flew by quickly, as it always did, and soon, we were back for the first day of school.

I had a different homeroom than the previous year, but I still had to go to that previous homeroom for a class later in the day, maybe English or social studies, which I can't recall. Over the summer, the janitorial staff had repainted all the walls, so the graffiti shrine was gone, covered by two layers of latex. As we waited for the previous class to end, I looked over at the wall and noticed a bump under the paint at the location where the booger was the prior year. Then I realized the painters never removed the offending loogie before painting; they simply painted over it! I mentioned this to several kids in line, who all got a great laugh out of it. Then, one of the kids took a marker, circled the bump, and wrote, "There's a booger under here." By the end of the day, more graffiti began filling the wall, including the insult about that poor guy Jim's lunch.

Again, some might find this story a bit disgusting (which it was), while others with a deeper appreciation for the bizarre (myself included) will see its irony and humor. I just consider it all part of "growin' up Skook."

121

Chapter 22

As I recall, we were all awestruck as we sat one Friday evening on our friend Dale's porch along North Ninth Street to see a parade of circus trucks and wagons traveling past, heading for the field behind the Ashland High School. We couldn't believe our eyes — a real, honest to God circus was in town.

Someone, I don't recall who, although it might have been one of the older boys attracted by the commotion, suggested we could volunteer to help them set up in the morning, and we might score a pair of free passes. This was too good to be true. Not only might we get to see a real, live circus, but if we helped set up, we would be right there in the mix. We'd be "up close and personal," as the TV news programs said.

Several of us followed the caravan along Ninth Street to the High School and then around to the field in the back. We found someone that looked like he might be in charge and asked if we could help. He wasn't a guy in ringmaster clothing wearing a top hat and a cape, but because he gave orders and told people where to park, we figured he might be important.

He told us that if we went home and got to bed early and could wake up at 4:00 am, we could come back and help. He said we would get free passes to see the circus if we did. We were all blown away. We headed home, told our parents, and got right to bed. You're probably wondering why parents would let their kids anywhere near a tribe of nomadic circus people. I don't really have a good answer other than these were different times. Also, I suspect our folks might have assumed local men from town would be around watching the activities.

Early the next morning, before the sun came up, several friends and I stood in the high school field watching teams of roustabouts raising one of the largest canvas tents I had ever seen. Then again, I had never previously seen a canvas tent of any size. When we slept out in our backyard on warm summer nights, it was in a tent made from blankets draped over two clotheslines and held together with clothespins. To say we were impressed was an understatement.

As we walked around trying to determine our assignments, we saw a man sitting on a wooden barrel, tying some knots with a rope. He was a black man, although people called men like him negroes back then. That is to say, that's how TV shows referred to people of color. In town, the more common term was a derogatory one, rarely used nowadays, the dreaded N-word. That's a word I have banished from my vocabulary, but that wasn't always the case.

I will beg your indulgence for the next few paragraphs. What I'm writing isn't to get cheap laughs or to ridicule anyone. It is simply to explain how things were and, thank goodness, no longer are. When we were kids, we tossed that N-word around like it was nothing; we were ignorant that it was offensive and simply didn't know any better. We learned from and mimicked older kids and our parents.

If you went to a candy store to buy licorice baby candies, you asked for "N-word" babies, and no one ever corrected us or told us we were doing something wrong. Girls playing jump rope chanting "Eanie, meanie, miney, moe" thought there was nothing wrong with saying, "Catch a 'N-word' by the toe." Unfortunately, it was a word that was commonly used.

In high school, one of my elderly English teachers was discussing our reading of Silas Marner. She tried explaining how the author told us something was wrong in one scene. She said, "In other words, he's saying there's a (N-word) in the wood pile." I had no idea then, or have no idea now, what that even meant. Reflecting on what she said from my hopefully somewhat enlightened adulthood, I can't believe a teacher would have said that in class. Those certainly were different times.

I had seen black people on television shows and in movies. The Little Rascals had Stymie and Buckwheat. There were often blacks on the Three Stooges, usually wide-eyed people scared by ghosts. My parents had several Harry Belafonte records. I asked once if he was a negro, and they explained that he was not. They said he was an "Islander." I was confused at the time, and then, in later years, I realized my parents enjoyed his music, but it wasn't a popular thing for townspeople to be associated with black folks in any capacity. Apparently, this "Islander" label was used to allow the act of listening to Mr. Belafonte to gain access to some understood loophole in the unspoken laws of bigoted social acceptance. I found it all very confusing.

In those days, there wasn't a single black family in town, so this black circus gentleman was my first live encounter with someone of his race. If this sounds like me assuming the roles of journalist Henry Morton Stanley and missionary David Livingstone on an adventure in Africa, I must apologize. But, I had never come face to face with any non-white person before, so this was something special for me.

We learned his name was Jim, and he was part of the traveling circus crew. I found this interesting because I had read Mark Twain's adventures with Tom Sawyer and Huck Finn, so I remembered Miss Watson had a slave named Jim. This disturbed me. Looking at this nice man, I couldn't imagine a time when people like him were bought and sold like property. It made me feel a bit guilty to be a white kid.

We asked Jim if we could help out, and he agreed. He and several other circus folks put us to work. I can't remember everything we did that day, but most of my time was spent setting up bleachers. That meant unloading dozens of heavy wooden planks from a truck, carrying them across the tent, and handing them off to men who placed them on risers for the public to watch the show. I had probably worked harder that day than I had ever worked in my young life, and I got plenty of blisters and splinters. As I recall, we never got our free passes when it was all said and done. That day taught me a valuable lesson about the types of people you can trust and those you can't. Apparently, carney folk are not the most trustworthy. Duh!

Another fantasy that was shattered in my young mind that day was the reality of the circus itself. On TV and in movies, circuses were presented as sparkling places of incredible fantasy, where everyone was beautiful, the tents were immaculate, the costumes were dazzling, and everyone was happy and cheerful. The reality I saw that day was one of worn, filthy, smelly canvas tents and people who looked exhausted, unhappy, and almost gray in appearance. I saw tattered and patched costumes that had lost any luster they might have had years earlier.

If the circuses of the movies were in bright, glorious colors, the circus in reality was a dismal black and white as viewed through a foggy lens. Instead of having the glory of something like the Emerald City in *The Wizard of Oz*, the real-life circus was more like a dystopian landscape one might see in an especially dark episode of The Twilight Zone. I realize this analogy might be a bit extreme, but let's just say my circus experience was not a favorable one.

On the positive side, I met my first black man and found the encounter enlightening. I've been a student of blues music for most of my adult life, a form of music introduced by black descendants of slaves. I'm happy to say I have left the negative racial aspects of "growin' up Skook" far behind me. If only the rest of those affected by racism could do the same.

126

Chapter 23

My dad was notorious for coming up with all sorts of expressions, many of which I have no idea where they originated. I assume, like me, he heard them, never questioned their meaning or purpose, accepted them at face value, and started using them because that's what people often do. The weird thing about some of these things was that they conveyed a message accurately while simultaneously defying logic. My father passed away more than thirty years ago, yet there are times I find myself saying, "I wish Dad were alive so maybe he could answer this question for me." I have found some answers online, but more often than not, I've come up empty-handed.

Here is one that baffles me. Most of us know about it, and many have used the services offered by a notary public at some time in our lives. We are sometimes called upon to have legal documents "officially notarized." For as long as I can remember, up until the day he died, my dad referred to notary publics as "Notary Joe Jacks." I have no idea why he used that term or where it came from. It might have been one of those terms so local that no one outside Schuylkill County heard of it. It could be even more localized than that. For example, I grew up calling a telephone pole a "telly pole," only to learn years later that this was a term seldom used outside my little town. I have scoured the internet, the source of all the knowledge in the known universe, but have not found the answer. I'm sure I will someday, but it remains a mystery to me for now.

Along the same lines was the word "stucon," or "stookon," or perhaps "stewcon;" I'm uncertain of the spelling as I have only heard the insult spoken. I heard my dad use it frequently when referring to someone who was really dumb. I, of course, knew the word "stupid" and was familiar with "moron." This made me wonder if "stucon" resulted from combining these two insults. Or was it possibly derived from one or more foreign words? With so many European nationalities melding together into one area, that might be where that answer lies. For now, it remains a mystery.

Sometimes, my father might have encountered someone he hadn't seen in some time and assumed by the way the person looked that he might be sickly or ill for some time. Perhaps the person had lost significant weight deliberately or due to being sick. When Dad described the person's appearance to us, he often would say, "He looked like death warmed over."

That certainly is an interesting concept, especially with the popularity of zombies over the past decade or so. How does someone warm over something dead? I got a bit luckier with this expression. I managed to find some references online. Some of them dated back to 1939. As it turned out, my dad used it exactly as it was meant to be used. I'd say that was one of those statements that, despite its complete lack of logic, still paints an accurate picture of such a sickly person's appearance.

Another expression Dad used to insult someone who obviously had no idea what he was saying was the vulgar gem, "He talks like a man with a paper asshole." Although clearly an insult, that one never made any physiological sense to me. I mean, no matter what material surrounded the orifice in question — whether paper, plastic, flesh, iron, glass, or steel — a hole was the absence of said material. Therefore, if the presence of a hole meant the absence of material, why should it matter what material originally was present and was now missing? With Dad gone, I assumed I might never discover the answer to this mystery.

However, as luck and investigative journalism would have it, I did find an internet reference that, although not exact, was close enough. The expression online was, "He talks like a man with a paper ass." This is described as meaning the person speaks superficially or insincerely. It is supposed that the idea of a "paper ass" suggests a weakness and a lack of legitimacy to the person's words.

128

I suspect the change from "ass" to "asshole" might have been my father's own modification to give the expression more punch and perhaps additional shock value. He had been known to exaggerate as necessary to get his point across. It explains my confusion about how a hole might have any physical structure. Okay, so maybe I was overthinking things a bit. Either way, I'm glad I never guessed, but I looked it up.

When we were little, my mom would ask my dad to take us driving at night during Christmas to see how people decorated their homes for the holiday. Although he would eventually agree to drive us, he would complain the whole time and say the houses looked like carnival wagons. I realized later that the reason he complained was likely because we could only afford to put up the minimum amount of lights, which usually consisted of one string around our front door.

At the time, I had no idea how his complaining would affect me in adulthood; however, my lovely wife has told me that on many occasions during our long marriage, I have used that same "carnival wagon" statement when looking at Christmas lights. For that, I apologize and ask forgiveness. The worst part of that story is I have no recollection of saying such a thing. I love looking at Christmas lights, but somehow, my dad's complaining must have found its way into my subconscious and out of my mouth.

Chapter 24

Many recollections from my childhood in Schuylkill County are not so much stories or anecdotes as they are glimpses, images, sensations, and vague remembrances. You might call them "this and that" or "odds and ends." They're not enough to merit separate chapters, but there might be tidbits worth mentioning just the same. In other words, to quote a song title from the late great singer/songwriter Jim Croce, they are "photographs and memories." However, they are much more than that, as these recollections can be triggered by a simple sound, smell, or other sensation. They are memories that pop out of thin air, brought forward by some unplanned stimulus.

If I think back to the summers of my childhood in the 1960s, one thing that always went hand in hand with summer was the sound of the Lokie whistle echoing through town. Ashland has a tourist attraction near the "toppa town" known as the Pioneer Tunnel Coal Mine tour, where you can ride to the bottom of an actual coal mine in passenger cars. Outside the mine on the surface is a steam locomotive called the Henry Clay, which takes passengers on a scenic trip around the mountain, with an excellent view of the town. This train is what we called the "Lokie," and its friendly whistle is one we grew to love and look forward to every spring and summer.

***

If I am walking around my neighborhood nowadays and smell paper burning, or if I am starting a fire in our outdoor firepit, my mind immediately flashes back to my childhood and the smells of the high school outdoor incinerator behind our house. That smell could guarantee that there would be a roaring fire in the cement block structure, busy burning that week's collection of test papers, confiscated magazines, and whatever other office debris required discarding. This was a time before paper shredders, so any important documents had to be burned. This made for a common smell in our neighborhood, one every kid there recognized. When you smelled the burning, you knew it was time to head to the incinerator, where your friends would likely be waiting, tossing sticks, leaves, and the like into the blazing fire, acting like wild pyromaniacal savages worshipping a fire god.

***

Another smell that I suppose I should consider revolting but brings back childhood memories is the sulfury smell of sewage. There's a reason for this, of course. In our neighborhood back when we were kids, there were several open-grated sewers around our streets, and for curious and bored kids, they were fascinating. You could stand on the grates, look down into the flowing groundwater, especially after heavy rain, and enjoy dropping rocks into it. Often, there were orange-colored deposits of sulfur along the edges of the stream. It had that distinct odor that I never forgot. Another fun thing to do was to watch the sewers from a distance and wait to see how many rats entered and exited them. We found our excitement wherever we could.

***

If I see a large hornet's nest in a tree, I am immediately reminded of an unpleasant episode from my youth. A gang of about ten of us were walking along a dirt road that ran next to my friend Eric's father's lumber mill, and we saw a huge hornet's nest in a tree along the road. It was more than a foot in diameter and was fairly low in the tree. We all knew that hornets were, by nature, miserable creatures, and they could become downright dangerous when threatened. Because of this, we opted to tread lightly past the ominous-looking nest, expecting to pass unscathed.

132

Suddenly, the last kid in line, a known troublemaker named Ricky, ran past all of us, shouting and laughing like a lunatic. Far too late, the rest of us realized what Ricky had done. He had hurled a huge rock at the hornet's nest, hitting it dead center and smashing it to bits, releasing hundreds of furious hornets in the process. Since Ricky was way ahead of us, he never was stung. The rest of us were not so lucky.

I can't recall who acquired the most stings, but I remember I had seven behind my left ear. I had swatted uselessly at the angry and now homeless hornets as they stung me repeatedly. I recall the area behind my ear becoming hot and swollen with a level of pain I will never forget.

***

When I feel the hot summer sun beating down on my mostly hairless head, I'm reminded to do something we never considered doing as kids — apply sunscreen. We never used any protection from the sun's rays, which is why many others of my generation and I regularly go to our dermatologist to be treated for skin issues that were a direct result of the sins of our youth. If anyone, usually girls, used lotion, its purpose wasn't to protect their skin from the sun's brutal rays but to get that "Coppertone" tan.

My oldest sister, Louise, had a sun exposure feature I looked forward to every summer. Her shoulders would burn and then peel. And by peel, I don't mean that flakey type of peel you could simply rub your palm across and brush off. I'm talking about long, wide sections of flesh that could be pulled off like a snake shedding its skin. Peels of several inches long were not unheard of. And the best part was she would let me do the peeling. I looked forward to peeling time every summer, hoping to beat the previous year's peel-a-thon in size and quantity. Now when I smell sunscreen, I'm thrust back in my mind to those wonderful and appealing (pun intended) times.

***

Back when I was learning to play guitar in the 1960s, I always hated what was known as "bubble gum music." For some reason, bands like the 1910 Fruit Gum Company with tinny organ-driven songs like Yummy, Yummy, Yummy, I Got Love In My Tummy and Simple Simon Says made me cringe, and I had no idea why. But I recall sitting at the high school baseball field, hanging with friends while watching a game, and hearing those obnoxious tunes pouring from transistor radios around me.

It's not that I was a music snob (although some who know me best might disagree) or that I was only listening to "cool" music; something about that bubble gum music felt wrong to me. Even a few years later, when made-up cartoon bands like The Archies or The Banana Splits came on the scene, they repulsed me. And in case you were wondering, The Monkees and The Partridge Family were never cool. So maybe I was/am a bit of a music snob.

Author's Notes

I hope you enjoyed the second volume of *Growin' Up Skook* and these memories. It was interesting and sometimes exhausting going back in time and remembering stories of my youth. People often ask me how I come up with my stories. My ideas for writing stories, whether fiction or nonfiction, are part of the internal dialog most writers and other creative types are blessed/cursed with. I recently read on the internet (so it *must* be true) that only between 30 percent and 50 percent of humans have a regular internal dialogue. By that, I mean having complete conversations inside their heads. I don't mean to confuse this with people who "hear voices" or who believe their dog tells them to do bad things. Those folks simply need a steady diet of Thorazine.

I'm referring to people who think not only in pictures and images, like most humans, but also those of us who have full conversations inside our heads most of our waking hours. We have to be careful when we start an actual verbal conversation with someone because that conversation may have already been going on in our minds before we even open our mouths. The result of this faux pax is obvious and immediate. The person you speak with looks at you like you just arrived on the shuttle from Mars and usually says, "I have no idea what you are talking about." Of course, it takes you a moment to realize they weren't involved in your imaginary conversation. Such is the world of someone living with an overactive mind.

Anyway, thanks for offering me whatever time it took you to read my stories. I hope you found them entertaining and well worth your precious time.

Thomas M. Malafarina

www.ingramcontent.com/pod-product-compliance
Lightning Source LLC
Chambersburg PA
CBHW070815100426
42742CB00012B/2364